POPULAR GOVERNMENT   *$7.95*

Sir Henry Sumner Maine's life spanned one of the most illustrious periods of English history, the Victorian Age. Not only was England the center of a vast empire and at its apex as a world power, the period is equally notable for its intellectual giants—Macaulay, Bagehot, Acton, Carlyle, Leslie and James Stephens, J. S. Mill, to name but a few. And no one compiling a list of the great scholars and intellects of this era could omit Sir Maine, whose contributions to the field of jurisprudence opened up new horizons and approaches for the comparative study of civilizations and their development.

Sir Maine is best remembered today for his seminal treatise, *Ancient Law*. Americans, however, should take particular interest in *Popular Government*, for it contains his celebrated essay on "The Constitution of the United States."

In his introduction, Professor Carey writes that "Sir Maine's largely favorable appraisal of the American system clearly indicates that he believed popular government was not only possible but, where conditions were appropriate, desirable. Yet history offers abundant proof of his overriding thesis: Popular governments, unless they are founded upon and consonant with the evolutionary development of a people, will crumble from their own excesses."

George W. Carey is Professor of Government at Georgetown University, and editor of *The Political Science Reviewer*. He is coauthor with Willmoore Kendall of *The Basic Symbols of the American Political Tradition*.

Sir Henry Sumner Maine

POPULAR GOVERNMENT

by SIR HENRY SUMNER MAINE

With an Introduction by
George W. Carey

LibertyClassics

INDIANAPOLIS

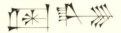
This edition of *Popular Government* follows the text of the edition published in London in 1885 by John Murray, Albemarle Street.

The cover art depicts Patrick Henry's speech to the Virginia House of Burgesses in May 1765, in which he declared: "Give me liberty or give me death!" Courtesy of the Patrick Henry Memorial Foundation, Brookneal, Virginia.

Library of Congress Catalog Card No.: 76-26329
ISBN 0-913966-14-2

CONTENTS

POPULAR GOVERNMENT

INTRODUCTION
by George W. Carey

Sir Henry Sumner Maine's life spanned one of the most illustrious periods of English history, the Victorian Age. Not only was England the center of a vast empire and at its apex as a world power, the period is equally notable for its intellectual giants—Macaulay, Bagehot, Acton, Carlyle, Leslie and James Stephens, J. S. Mill, to name but a few. And no one compiling a list of the great scholars and intellects of this extraordinary era could omit Sir Maine, whose contributions to the field of jurisprudence opened up new horizons and approaches for the comparative study of civilizations and their development. Nor could one interested in the great affairs of the British Empire ignore his contributions to the administration of India.

Sir Maine's life most certainly was not adventurous or particularly intriguing. Quite the contrary. One might say his life was a series of steady and purposive accomplishments, wherein each stage seemed to follow logically on the preceding.

He was born in 1822 near Leighton, Scotland. After the separation of his parents, his mother took him to reside with her at Henley-on-Thames. In 1829, through the efforts of his godfather—who was Bishop of Chester—he was admitted to Christ's Hospital, where he soon distinguished himself as a very gifted student. In 1840 he was to enter Pembroke College, Cambridge, as an Exhibitioner of Christ's Hospital.

His achievements at Cambridge were most remarkable. In addition to winning honors for his Greek and Latin compositions and English verses, he was elected a Foundation Scholar (1841), a Craven University Scholar (1843), and was awarded the Senior Classics Medal (1844), the highest university honor. In 1844 he accepted the position of Tutor of Trinity Hall, Cambridge Law College, serving in this capacity until 1847, when he was appointed Regius Professor of Civil Law.

In the early 1850s, Sir Maine was to undertake the practice of law but his health, always quite delicate from early youth, would not permit him to pursue a practicing legal career with vigor. More important in light of his subsequent career was his appointment in 1852 to the Inns of Court, the London legal center, where he lectured on the subject of Roman Law and Jurisprudence. From these lectures emerged *Ancient Law* (1861), his most famous and celebrated work. This book, coupled with his contributions, more or less regular, to the *Saturday Review,* established his reputation not only as a juridical scholar of the first order but also as a knowledgeable individual with keen perceptions concerning contemporary social and political movements.

Soon after the appearance of *Ancient Law,* his career was to take a somewhat different direction. With some reluctance, this owing largely to his frail health, he accepted appointment as the Law Member of the Council of Governor-General of India. His duties principally involved reform and codification of Indian law and provided him with the opportunity to apply in practice principles which he had set forth in *Ancient Law.* He served in this capacity until 1869.

Upon his return to England, Sir Maine was named Corpus Professor of Jurisprudence at Oxford, thus becoming the first professor of comparative jurisprudence in Oxford's history. Shortly thereafter (1871), he was named Knight Commander of the Star of India and appointed as a permanent and paid member to the Council of the Secretary of State for India. Despite his work with the Indian Council, his tenure at Oxford was a most productive one. He produced three books based largely on his Oxford lectures: *Village Communities in the East and West* (1871); *Lectures on the Early History of Institutions* (1875); and *Dissertations on Early Law and Custom* (1883).

In 1878, Sir Maine was to return to Cambridge as Master of Trinity College, a position which allowed him to devote more attention to Indian Council affairs. However, he still contributed frequently to periodic journals. Certain of these articles which first appeared in the *Quarterly Review* form the corpus of his *Popular Government* (1885). His final work, posthumously published, was *International Law,* based upon his lectures at Cambridge as Whewell Professor of International Law, a position to which he was appointed in 1887.

Sir Maine died of cerebral hemorrhage in Cannes, France, on February 3, 1888.

While there can be no doubt that Sir Maine's activities did have an impact on his times, particularly with respect to the affairs of India, his more lasting contribution is to be found in his principal writings. The most celebrated of these, as previously mentioned, is *Ancient Law* because it stands as a pioneering effort in the study of the source and growth of law. "If by any means," he wrote in the opening passages of this work, "we can determine the early forms of jural conceptions, they will be invaluable to us. The rudimentary ideas are to the jurist what the primary crusts of the earth are to the geologist. They contain, potentially, all the forms in which law has subsequently exhibited itself."[1] And, using principally Roman Law as his reference point, he was able to trace the evolution of major aspects of the law (e.g., property, contract, criminal, wills and succession) from the earliest times forward, simultaneously showing how modern legal conceptions and codes are the outgrowth of the slow and gradual development of ancient conceptions and fictions. Because of its approach, *Ancient Law* is frequently compared with Darwin's *Origin of Species.*

However notable for its approach, *Ancient Law* advanced certain propositions which are of importance for understanding his later works and theory. Perhaps the best known of these is the general formulation that "the movement of the progressive societies has hitherto been

---

[1] Sir Henry Sumner Maine, *Ancient Law* (New York: E. P. Dutton and Co., 1917), p. 2.

a movement *from Status to Contract.*"[2] He meant by this, to put the matter simply, that ancient law was concerned with the specification of relationships between what can be termed extended families, not individuals. In this order of things, individual members of the family were completely subject to the control of the family head. For example, as embodied in the Roman legal conception, *Patria Potestas,* the head of the family possessed within his realm the power of life and death, the authority to arrange marriages and issue divorces and, among others, the right to sell his children. Thus the status of the individual was completely defined in the context of this patriarchal authority.

The movement to contract, the mark of the more progressive societies, involved in its most important dimension the breakdown of *Patria Potestas* and the recognition of the capacity of individuals to assume powers, responsibilities, and authority which previously were only within the province of the family head. Thus, contractual relationships between emancipated individuals, a condition duly reflected in the legal codes of civilized states, is the central focus of modern jurisprudence. But, as Sir Maine was careful to point out, modern jurisprudence in no small degree still employs those forms and concepts which were utilized, albeit in far less refined form, in the ancient laws.

Sir Maine's observations concerning the character and evolution of the law of nature also deserve comment. From the earliest times forward, all societies, he noted, have possessed concepts of higher ideals to which posi-

---

[2] *Ibid.,* p. 100.

tive law and its applications ought to conform. Yet, two major difficulties have arisen both in ancient and modern times regarding the relationship of "higher" or ideal law and positive or man-made law. First, the higher law may become so dominant that little heed is paid to the settled prescriptions or rules of society. More exactly, various interpretations of the higher law may be superimposed on an *ad hoc* basis in the settlement of conflict, a situation hardly conducive to the permanency, stability, or consistency of the legal codes and their meaning. Societies which have been plagued by this difficulty (the foremost of which were the ancient Greek) present the modern observer with no coherent jurisprudence, rather a legacy which informs us only of the different priorities accorded the elements of the higher law at different times.

A second and seemingly more serious difficulty which he perceived was this: "Higher law" may operate in such a fashion as to stifle the progress of a civilization. This occurs when a people look over their shoulders, so to speak, and associate the higher law with the principles upon which the original laws were codified. And this, in large measure, was the situation that Sir Maine confronted in India.

In Sir Maine's estimation, the status accorded the law of nature in Roman times avoided both pitfalls. While, indeed, there were conceptions of a higher law, these conceptions were seldom, if ever, allowed to supersede the strictures and commands of man-made law. The higher law was not perceived as standing in an antagonistic relationship to the positive law and could best be discovered or approximated through evolutionary refinement, a gradual process that would eventually yield up or reveal the essence or underlying principles of seemingly diverse and disparate positive laws. In Sir Maine's words, the notion prevailed that the law of nature "underlay existing law and must be looked for through it." The principal function of the natural law in this context was "remedial, not revolutionary or anarchical."[3]

These elements of his thinking should be borne in mind by those who want to place *Popular Government* in its proper perspective, the more so as critics over the years have sought to drive a wedge between it and *Ancient Law.* Some critics allege that in writing *Popular Government* he allowed his political beliefs and prejudices to divert him from the path of sound scholarship. Sir Ernest Barker writes, "the final upshot of the Historical Method, if we turn to *Popular Government,* seems to be a somewhat melancholy conservatism."[4] Another critic puts the matter this way: "Maine's violation of the scientific method or of ordinary reasoning shows perhaps more than anything else the strength of his conservatism."[5]

Nevertheless, *Popular Government* by any standard is only a rational extension and application of the findings so carefully, logically, and painstakingly developed in *Ancient Law.* In short, there is no gulf or cleavage between these works. In both he shows a keen awareness of the absurdities connected with natural law theories (princi-

---

[3] *Ibid.,* p. 45.

[4] Sir Ernest Barker, *Political Thought in England, 1848-1914* (New York: Oxford University Press, 1959), p. 145.

[5] Benjamin Evans Lippincott, *Victorian Critics of Democracy* (Minneapolis: University of Minnesota Press, 1938), p. 199.

pally Rousseau's) based upon a fictitious and prehistoric
state of nature characterized by extreme individualism.
Moreover, in both books he emphasizes that the utilitari-
anism of Bentham represents but a pitiful perversion of
the ancient notions of natural law. To be sure, in *Popular
Government* he is more immediately concerned with the
acceptance and application of these false theories because
of their central role in democratic ideology. Yet any per-
ceptive reader of *Ancient Law* can certainly see the logic
and validity of his approach and emphasis in *Popular Government,* as well as its timeliness since the forces of demo-
cratism in Victorian England were in the ascendancy.

To regard *Popular Government,* then, as merely a partisan
attack on democracy and popular governments in general
would be a gross mistake. Sir Maine's largely favorable
appraisal of the American system clearly indicates that
he believed popular government was not only possible
but, where conditions were appropriate, desirable. And
history offers abundant proof of his overriding thesis:
Popular governments, unless they are founded upon and
consonant with the evolutionary development of a people, will crumble from their own excesses. In this sense,
to quote Peter Viereck, *"Popular Government* systematized
the Burkean approach into a consistent philosophy"[6]
fully suited for modern conditions. But this Sir Maine
was only able to do because, like Burke, he heeded the
wisdom of the ages.

----

[6] Peter Viereck, *Conservatism from John Adams to Churchill* (Princeton, N.J.: D. Van
Nostrand and Co., 1956), p. 32.

PREFACE

The four Essays which follow are connected with studies to which, during much of my life, I have devoted such leisure as I have been able to command. Many years ago I made the attempt, in a work on *Ancient Law,* to apply the so-called Historical Method of inquiry to the private laws and institutions of Mankind. But, at the outset of this undertaking, I found the path obstructed by a number of *à priori* theories which, in all minds but a few, satisfied curiosity as to the Past and paralysed speculation as to the Future. They had for their basis the hypothesis of a Law and State of Nature antecedent to all positive institutions, and a hypothetical system of Rights and Duties appropriate to the natural condition. The gradual recovery of the natural condition was assumed to be the same thing as the progressive improvement of human institutions. Upon the examination, which was indispensable, of the true origin and real history of these theories, I found them to rest upon a very slender philosophical foundation, but at the same time they might be shown to have been extremely powerful both for good and evil. One of the characteristics most definitely associated with Nature and her Law was simplicity, and thus the theories of which I am speaking brought about (though less in England than in other countries) many valuable reforms of private law, by simplifying it and clearing it from barbarous technicalities. They had, further, a large share in the parentage of International Law, and they thus helped to mitigate in some small degree the sanguinary quarrelsomeness which has accompanied the human race through the whole course of its history. But, on the other hand, they in my judgment unnerved the human intellect, and thus made it capable of the extravagances into which it fell at the close of the eighteenth century. And they certainly gave a false bias to all historical inquiry into the growth of society and the development of law.

It has always been my desire and hope to apply the Historical Method to the political institutions of men. But, here again, the inquiry into the history of these institutions, and the attempt to estimate their true value by the results of such an inquiry, are seriously embarrassed by a mass of ideas and beliefs which have grown up in our day on the subject of one particular form of government, that extreme form of popular government which is called Democracy. A portion of the notions which prevail in Europe concerning Popular Government are derived (and these are worthy of all respect) from observation of its practical working; a larger portion merely reproduce technical rules of the British or American constitutions in an altered or disguised form; but a multitude of ideas on this subject, ideas which are steadily absorbing or displacing all others, appear to me, like the theories of jurisprudence of which I have spoken, to have been conceived *à priori*. They are, in fact, another set of deductions from the assumption of a State of Nature. Their true source has never been forgotten on the Continent of Europe, where they are well known to have sprung from the teaching of Jean-Jacques Rousseau, who believed that men emerged from the primitive natural condition by a process which made every form of government, except Democracy, illegitimate. In this country they are not often explicitly, or even consciously, referred to their real origin, which is, nevertheless, constantly betrayed by the language in which they are expressed. Democracy is commonly described as having an inherent superiority over every other form of government. It is supposed to advance with an irresistible and preordained movement. It is thought to be full of the promise of blessings to mankind; yet if it fails to bring with it these blessings, or even proves to be prolific of the heaviest calamities, it is not held to deserve condemnation. These are the familiar marks of a theory which claims to be independent of experience and observation on the plea that it bears the credentials of a golden age, non-historical and unverifiable.

During the half-century in which an *à priori* political theory has been making way among all the civilised societies of the West, a set of political facts have disclosed themselves by its side which appear to me to deserve much more consideration than they have received. Sixty or seventy years ago, it was inevitable that an inquirer into political science should mainly employ the deductive

method of investigation. Jeremy Bentham, who was careless of remote history, had little before him beyond the
phenomena of the British Constitution, which he saw in
the special light of his own philosophy and from the point
of view of a reformer of private law. Besides these he had
a few facts supplied by the short American Constitutional
experience, and he had the brief and most unsuccessful
experiments of the French in democratic government. But
since 1815, and especially since 1830, Popular Government has been introduced into nearly all Continental
Europe and into all Spanish America, North, Central, and
South; and the working of these new institutions has
furnished us with a number of facts of the highest interest. Meantime, the ancient British Constitution has been
modifying itself with a rapidity which could not be foreseen in Bentham's day. I suspect that there were few
observant Englishmen who, in presence of the agitation
which filled the summer and autumn of 1884, were not
astonished to discover the extent to which the Constitution of their country had altered, under cover of old language and old forms. And, all the while, the great strength
of some of the securities which the American Federal
Constitution has provided against the infirmities of
popular government has been proving itself in a most
remarkable way. Thus, in nearly all the civilised world,
a large body of new facts has been formed by which I
endeavour, in these Essays, to test the value of the opinions which are gaining currency in our day concerning
Popular Government as it verges on Democracy.

It would argue ignorance or bad faith to deny the bene-
fits for which, amid some calamities, mankind is indebted
to Popular Government. Nevertheless, if there be even an

approximation to truth in the conclusions which I have reached in the three papers first printed in this volume, some assumptions commonly made on the subject must be discarded. In the Essay on the "Prospects of Popular Government" I have shown that, as a matter of fact, Popular Government, since its reintroduction into the world, has proved itself to be extremely fragile. In the Essay on the "Nature of Democracy" I have given some reasons for thinking that, in the extreme form to which it tends, it is, of all kinds of government, by far the most difficult. In the "Age of Progress" I have argued that the perpetual change which, as understood in modern times, it appears to demand, is not in harmony with the normal forces ruling human nature, and is apt therefore to lead to cruel disappointment or serious disaster. If I am in any degree right, Popular Government, especially as it approaches the democratic form, will tax to the utmost all the political sagacity and statesmanship of the world to keep it from misfortune. Happily, if there are some facts which augur ill for its duration and success, there are others which suggest that it is not beyond the powers of human reason to discover remedies for its infirmities. For the purpose of bringing out a certain number of these latter facts, and at the same time of indicating the quarter in which the political student (once set free from *à priori* assumptions) may seek materials for a reconstruction of his science, I have examined and analysed the Constitution of the United States, a topic on which much misconception seems to be abroad. There are some who appear to suppose that it sprang at once from the brain like the Goddess of Wisdom, an idea very much in harmony with modern Continental fancies respecting the origin of Democracy. I have tried to show that its birth was in reality natural, from ordinary historical antecedents; and that its connection with wisdom lay in the skill with which sagacious men, conscious that certain weaknesses which it had inherited would be aggravated by the new circumstances in which it would be placed, provided it with appliances calculated to minimise them or to neutralise them altogether. Its success, and the success of such American institutions as have succeeded, appears to me to have arisen rather from skilfully applying the curb to popular impulses than from giving them the rein. While the British Constitution has been insensibly transforming itself into a popular government surrounded on all sides by difficulties, the American Federal Constitution has proved that, nearly a century ago, several expedients were discovered by which some of these difficulties may be greatly mitigated and some altogether overcome.

The publication of the substance of these Essays in the *Quarterly Review,* besides giving me a larger audience than could be expected for a dissertation on abstract and general Politics which had little direct bearing on the eager controversies of Party, has gained for me the further advantage of a number of criticisms which reached me before this volume took its final shape. At the head of these I must place a series of observations with which Lord Acton has favoured me. I have freely availed myself of these results of his great learning and profound thought.

H. S. Maine

London, 1885

ESSAY I

THE PROSPECTS OF POPULAR
GOVERNMENT

The blindness of the privileged classes in France to the Revolution which was about to overwhelm them furnishes some of the best-worn commonplaces of modern history. There was no doubt much in it to surprise us. What King, Noble, and Priest could not see, had been easily visible to the foreign observer. "In short," runs the famous passage in Chesterfield's letter of December 25, 1753, "all the symptoms which I ever met with in history previous to great changes and revolutions in government now exist and daily increase in France." A large number of writers of our day, manifesting the wisdom which comes after the event, have pointed out that the signs of a terrible time ought not to have been mistaken. The Court, the Aristocracy, and the Clergy should have understood that, in face of the irreligion which was daily becoming more fashionable, the belief in privilege conferred by birth could not be long maintained. They should have noted the portents of imminent political disturbance in the intense jealousy of classes. They should have been prepared for a tremendous social upheaval by the squalor and misery of the peasants. They should have observed the immediate causes of revolution in the disorder of the finances and in the gross inequality of taxation. They should have been wise enough to know that the entire structure, of which the keystone was a stately and scandalous Court, was undermined on all sides. "Beautiful Armida Palace, where the inmates live enchanted lives; lapped in soft music of adulation; waited on by the splendours of the world; which nevertheless hangs wondrously as by a single hair."[1]

But although Chesterfield appeals to history, the careful modern student of history will perhaps think the blindness of the French nobility and clergy eminently pardonable. The Monarchy, under whose broad shelter all privilege grew and seemed to thrive, appeared to have its roots deeper in the past than any existing European institution. The countries which now made up France had enjoyed no experience of popular government since the rude Gaulish freedom. From this, they had passed into the condition of a strictly administered, strongly governed, highly taxed, Roman province. The investigations of the young and learned school of historians rising in France leave it questionable whether the Germans, who are sometimes supposed to have redeemed their own barbarism by reviving liberty, brought anything like freedom to Gaul. There was little more than a succession of German to Roman privileged classes. German captains

---

[1] Carlyle, *French Revolution,* i. 4.

shared the great estates, and assumed the rank, of the half-official, half-hereditary nobility, who abounded in the province. A German King, who was in reality only a Roman general bearing a barbarous title, reigned over much of Gaul and much of Central Europe. When his race was supplanted by another in its kingship, the new power got itself decorated with the old Roman Imperial style; and when at length a third dynasty arose, the monarchy associated with it gradually developed more vigour and vitality than any other political institution in Europe. From the accession of Hugh Capet to the French Revolution, there had been as nearly as possible 800 years. During all this time, the French Royal House had steadily gained in power. It had wearied out and beaten back the victorious armies of England. It had emerged stronger than ever from the wars of religion which humbled English kingship in the dust, dealing it a blow from which it never thoroughly recovered. It had grown in strength, authority, and splendour, till it dazzled all eyes. It had become the model for all princes. Nor had its government and its relation to its subjects struck all men as they seem to have struck Chesterfield. Eleven years before Chesterfield wrote, David Hume, a careful observer of France, had thus written in 1742, "Though all kinds of government be improved in modern times, yet monarchical government seems to have made the greatest advance to perfection. It may now be affirmed of civilised monarchies, what was formerly said of republics alone, that they are a government of laws, not of men. They are found susceptible of order, method, and constancy, to a surprising degree. Property is there secure; industry is encouraged;

the arts flourish; and the Prince lives among his subjects like a father among his children." And Hume expressly adds that he saw more "sources of degeneracy" in free governments like England than in France, "the most perfect model of pure monarchy."[2]

Nevertheless, Hume was unquestionably wrong in his conclusion, and Chesterfield was as unquestionably right. The French privileged classes might conceivably have foreseen the great Revolution, simply because it happened. The time, however, which is expended in wondering at their blindness, or in pitying it with an air of superior wisdom, is as nearly as possible wasted. Next to what a modern satirist has called "Hypothetics"—the science of that which might have happened but did not— there is no more unprofitable study than the investigation of the possibly predictable, which was never predicted. It is of far higher advantage to note the mental condition of the French upper classes as one of the most remarkable facts in history, and to ask ourselves whether it conveys a caution to other generations than theirs. This line of speculation is at the least interesting. We too, who belong to Western Europe towards the end of the nineteenth century, live under a set of institutions which all, except a small minority, regard as likely to be perpetual. Nine men out of ten, some hoping, some fearing, look upon the popular government which, ever widening its basis, has spread and is still spreading over the world, as destined to last for ever, or, if it changes its form, to change it in one single direction. The democratic principle has gone

---

[2] Hume, Essay XII, *Of Civil Liberty.*

forth conquering and to conquer, and its gainsayers are
few and feeble. Some Catholics, from whose minds the
diplomacy of the present Pope has not banished the Syl-
labus of the last, a fairly large body of French and Spanish
Legitimists, and a few aged courtiers in the small circles
surrounding exiled German and Italian princes, may still
believe that the cloud of democratic ascendency will pass
away. Their hopes may be as vain as their regrets; but
nevertheless those who recollect the surprises which the
future had in store for men equally confident in the perpetuity of the present, will ask themselves whether it is
really true that the expectation of virtual permanence for
governments of the modern type rests upon solid grounds
of historical experience as regards the past, and of rational
probability as regards the time to come. I endeavour in
these pages to examine the question in a spirit different
from that which animates most of those who view the
advent of democracy either with enthusiasm or with despair.

Out of the many names commonly applied to the
political system prevailing or tending to prevail in all the
civilised portions of the world, I have chosen "popular
government"[3] as the name which, on the whole, is least
open to objection. But what we are witnessing in West
European politics is not so much the establishment of a
definite system, as the continuance, at varying rates, of
a process. The truth is that, within two hundred years,

---

[3] It will be seen that I endeavour to use the term "democracy," throughout
this volume, in its proper and only consistent sense; that is, for a particular
form of government.

the view taken of government, or (as the jurists say) of the relation of sovereign to subject, of political superior to political inferior, has been changing, sometimes partially and slowly, sometimes generally and rapidly. The character of this change has been described by John Stuart Mill in the early pages of his "Essay on Liberty," and more recently by Mr. Justice Stephen, who in his *History of the Criminal Law of England* very strikingly uses the contrast between the old and the new view of government to illustrate the difference between two views of the law of seditious libel. I will quote the latter passage as less coloured than the language of Mill by the special preferences of the writer:

> Two different views may be taken [says Sir James Stephen] of the relation between rulers and their subjects. If the ruler is regarded as the superior of the subject, as being by the nature of his position presumably wise and good, the rightful ruler and guide of the whole population, it must necessarily follow that it is wrong to censure him openly, and, even if he is mistaken, his mistakes should be pointed out with the utmost respect, and that, whether mistaken or not, no censure should be cast on him likely or designed to diminish his authority. If, on the other hand, the ruler is regarded as the agent and servant, and the subject as the wise and good master, who is obliged to delegate his power to the so-called ruler because, being a multitude, he cannot use it himself, it must be evident that this sentiment must be reversed. Every member of the public who censures the ruler for the time being exercises in his own person the right which belongs to the whole of which he forms a part. He is finding fault with his own servant.[4]

The States of Europe are now regulated by political institutions answering to the various stages of the transi-

---

[4] Stephen's *History of the Criminal Law of England,* ii. 299.

tion from the old view, that "rulers are presumably wise and good, the rightful rulers and guides of the whole population," to the newer view, that "the ruler is the agent and servant, and the subject the wise and good master, who is obliged to delegate his power to the so-called ruler because, being a multitude, he cannot use it himself." Russia and Turkey are the only European States which completely reject the theory that governments hold their powers by delegation from the community, the word "community" being somewhat vaguely understood, but tending more and more to mean at least the whole of the males of full age living within certain territorial limits. This theory, which is known on the Continent as the theory of national sovereignty, has been fully accepted in France, Italy, Spain, Portugal, Holland, Belgium, Greece, and the Scandinavian States. In Germany it has been repeatedly repudiated by the Emperor and his powerful Minister, but it is to a very great extent acted upon. England, as is not unusual with her, stands by herself. There is no country in which the newer view of government is more thoroughly applied to practice, but almost all the language of the law and constitution is still accommodated to the older ideas concerning the relation of ruler and subject.

But, although no such inference could be drawn from English legal phraseology, there is no doubt that the modern popular government of our day is of purely English origin. When it came into existence, there were Republics in Europe, but they exercised no moral and little political influence. Although in point of fact they were most of them strict oligarchies, they were regarded as somewhat plebeian governments, over which monarchies took rightful precedence. "The Republics in Europe," writes Hume in 1742, "are at present noted for want of politeness. The good manners of a Swiss civilised in Holland is an expression for rusticity among the French. The English is some degree fall under the same censure, notwithstanding their learning and genius. And if the Venetians be an exception, they owe it perhaps to their communication with other Italians." If a man then called himself a Republican, he was thinking of the Athenian or Roman Republic, one for a while in a certain sense a democracy, the other from first to last an aristocracy, but both ruling a dependent empire with the utmost severity. In reality, the new principle of government was solely established in England, which Hume always classes with Republics rather than with Monarchies. After tremendous civil struggles, the doctrine that governments serve the community was, in spirit if not in words, affirmed in 1689. But it was long before this doctrine was either fully carried out by the nation or fully accepted by its rulers. William III was merely a foreign politician and general, who submitted to the eccentricities of his subjects for the sake of using their wealth and arms in foreign war. On this point the admissions of Macaulay are curiously in harmony with the view of William taken in the instructions of Louis XIV to his diplomatists which have lately been published. Anne certainly believed in her own quasi-divine right; and George I and George II were humbler kings of the same type as William, who thought that the proper and legitimate form of government was to be found, not in England, but in Hanover. As soon as England had in George III a king who cared more for English politics than for foreign war, he repudiated the doctrine altogether; nor can it be said that it was really admitted by any English sovereign until, possibly, the present reign. But even when the horror of the French Revolution was at its highest, the politician, who would have been in much danger of prosecution if he had toasted the People as the "sole legitimate source of power," could always save himself by drinking to "the principles which placed the House of Hanover on the throne." These principles in the meantime were more and more becoming the actual rule of government, and before George III died they had begun their victorious march over Europe.

Popular government, as first known to the English, began to command the interest of the Continent through the admiration with which it inspired a certain set of French thinkers towards the middle of the last century. At the outset, it was not English Liberty which attracted them, but English Toleration and also English Irreligion, the last one of the most fugitive phases through which the mind of a portion of the nation passed, but one which so struck the foreign observer that, at the beginning of the present century, we find Napoleon Bonaparte claiming the assistance of the Pope as rightfully his because he was the enemy of the British misbeliever. Gradually the educated classes of France, at whose feet sat the educated class of all Continental countries, came to interest themselves in English political institutions; and then came two events, one of which greatly encouraged, while the other in the end greatly discouraged, the tendency of popular government to diffuse itself. The first of them was the foundation of the United States. The American

Constitution is distinctively English; this might be proved alone, as Mr. Freeman has acutely observed, by its taking two Houses, instead of one, or three, or more, as the normal structure of a legislative assembly. It is in fact the English Constitution carefully adapted to a body of Englishmen who had never had much to do with an hereditary king and an aristocracy of birth, and who had determined to dispense with them altogether. The American Republic has greatly influenced the favour into which popular government grew. It disproved the once universal assumptions, that no Republic could govern a large territory, and that no strictly Republican government could be stable. But at first the Republic became interesting for other reasons. It now became possible for Continental Europeans to admire popular government without submitting to the somewhat bitter necessity of admiring the English, who till lately had been the most unpopular of European nations. Frenchmen in particular, who had helped and perhaps enabled the Americans to obtain their independence, naturally admired institutions which were indirectly their own creation; and Frenchmen who had not served in the American War saw the American freeman reflected in Franklin, who pleased the school of Voltaire because he believed nothing, and the school of Rousseau because he wore a Quaker coat. The other event strongly influencing the fortunes of popular government was the French Revolution, which in the long-run rendered it an object of horror. The French, in their new Constitutions, followed first the English and then the American model, but in both cases with large departures from the originals. The result in both cases was miserable miscarriage. Political liberty took long to recover from the discredit into which it had been plunged by the Reign of Terror. In England, detestation of the Revolution did not cease to influence politics till 1830. But, abroad, there was a reaction to the older type of popular government in 1814 and 1815; and it was thought possible to combine freedom and order by copying, with very slight changes, the British Constitution. From a longing for liberty, combined with a loathing of the French experiments in it, there sprang the state of opinion in which the constitutional movements of the Continent had their birth. The British political model was followed by France, by Spain and Portugal, and by Holland and Belgium, combined in the kingdom of the Netherlands; and, after a long interval, by Germany, Italy, and Austria.

The principle of modern popular government was thus affirmed less than two centuries ago, and the practical application of that principle outside these islands and their dependencies is not quite a century old. What has been the political history of the commonwealths in which this principle has been carried out in various degrees? The inquiry is obviously one of much importance and interest; but, though the materials for it are easily obtained, and indeed are to a large extent within the memory of living men, it is very seldom or very imperfectly prosecuted. I undertake it solely with the view of ascertaining, within reasonable limits of space, how far actual experience countenances the common assumption of our day, that popular government is likely to be of indefinitely long duration. I will first take France, which began with the imitation of the English, and has ended with the adoption of the American model. Since the introduction of political freedom into France, the existing government, nominally clothed with all the powers of the State, has been three times overturned by the mob of Paris, in 1792, in 1830, and in 1848. It has been three times overthrown by the Army; first in 1797, on the 4th of September (18 Fructidor), when the majority of the Directors with the help of the soldiery annulled the elections of forty-eight departments, and deported fifty-six members of the two Assemblies, condemning also to deportation two of their own colleagues. The second military revolution was effected by the elder Bonaparte on the 9th of November (18 Brumaire), 1799; and the third by the younger Bonaparte, on December 2, 1851. The French Government has also been three times destroyed by foreign invasion, in 1814, 1815, and 1870; the invasion having been in each case provoked by French aggression, sympathised in by the bulk of the French people. In all, putting aside the anomalous period from 1870 to 1885, France, since she began her political experiments, has had forty-four years of liberty and thirty-seven of stern dictatorship.[5] But it has to be remembered, and it is one of the curiosities of this period of history, that the elder Bourbons, who in practice gave very wide room to political freedom, did not expressly admit the modern theory of popular government; while the Bonapartes, who proclaimed the theory without qualification, maintained in practice a rigid despotism.

---

[5] I include in the thirty-seven years the interval between September 1797 and November 1799.

Popular government was introduced into Spain just when the fortune of war was declaring itself decisively in favour of Wellington and the English army. The Extraordinary Cortes signed at Cadiz a Constitution, since then famous in Spanish politics as the Constitution of 1812, which proclaimed in its first article that sovereignty resided in the nation. Ferdinand VII, on re-entering Spain from France, repudiated this Constitution, denouncing it as Jacobinical; and for about six years he reigned as absolutely as any of his forefathers. But in 1820 General Riego, who was in command of a large force stationed near Cadiz, headed a military insurrection in which the mob joined; and the King submitted to the Constitution of 1812. In 1823 the foreign invader appeared; the French armies entered Spain at the instigation of the Holy Alliance, and re-established Ferdinand's despotism, which lasted till his death. Popular government was, however, reintroduced by his widow as Regent for his daughter, no doubt for the purpose of strengthening Isabella's title to the throne against her uncle, Don Carlos. It is probably unnecessary to give the subsequent political history of Spain in any detail. There are some places in South America where the people date events, not from the great earthquakes, but from the years in which, by a rare intermission, there is no earthquake at all. On the same principle we may note that during the nine years following 1845, and the nine years following 1857, there was comparative, though not complete, freedom from military insurrection in Spain. As to the residue of her political history, my calculation is that between the first establishment of popular government in 1812 and the accession

of the present King, there have been forty military risings
of a serious nature, in most of which the mob took part.
Nine of them were perfectly successful, either over-
throwing the Constitution for the time being, or reversing
the principles on which it was administered. I need hardly
say that both the Queen Regent, Christina, and her
daughter Isabella, were driven out of Spain by the army
or the fleet, with the help of the mob; and that the present
King, Alfonso, was placed on the throne through a military *pronunciamento* at the end of 1874. It is generally
thought that he owes his retention of it since 1875 to
statesmanship of a novel kind. As soon as he has assured
himself that the army is in earnest, he changes his ministers.

The real beginning of popular or parliamentary government in Germany and the Austrian dominions, other than
Hungary, cannot be placed earlier than 1848. The interest
of German politics from 1815 to that year consists in the
complaints, ever growing fainter, of the German communities who sought to compel the Princes to redeem their
promises of Constitutions made during the War of Independence, and of the efforts of the Princes to escape
or evade their pledges. Francis the Second expressed the
prevailing feeling in his own way when he said to the
Hungarian Diet, "totus mundus stultizat, et vult habere
novas constitutiones." With some exceptions in the
smaller States there were no parliamentary institutions in
Germany till the King of Prussia conceded, just before
1848, the singular form of constitutional government
which did not survive that year. But as soon as the mob
of Paris had torn up the French Constitutional Charter,

and expelled the Constitutional King, mobs, with their
usual accompaniment the army, began to influence German and even Austrian politics. National Assemblies, on
the French pattern, were called together at Berlin, at
Vienna, and at Frankfurt. All of them were dispersed in
about a year, and directly or indirectly by the army. The
more recent German and Austrian Constitutions are all
of royal origin. Taking Europe as a whole, the most dura-
bly successful experiments in popular government have
been made either in small States, too weak for foreign
war, such as Holland and Belgium, or in countries, like
the Scandinavian States, where there was an old tradition
of political freedom. The ancient Hungarian Constitution
has been too much affected by civil war for any assertion
about it to be safe. Portugal, for a while scarcely less
troubled than Spain by military insurrection, has been
free from it of late; and Greece has had the dynasty of
her kings once changed by revolution.

If we look outside Europe and beyond the circle of
British dependencies, the phenomena are much the same.
The civil war of 1861–65, in the United States, was as
much a war of revolution as the war of 1775–1782. It was
a war carried on by the adherents of one set of principles
and one construction of the Constitution against the adherents of another body of principles and another Constitutional doctrine. It would be absurd, however, to deny
the relative stability of the Government of the United
States, which is a political fact of the first importance; but
the inferences which might be drawn from it are much
weakened, if not destroyed, by the remarkable spectacle
furnished by the numerous republics set up from the

Mexican border-line to the Straits of Magellan. It would take many of these pages even to summarise the whole political history of the Spanish-American communities. There have been entire periods of years during which some of them have been disputed between the multitude and the military, and again when tyrants, as brutal as Caligula or Commodus, reigned over them like a Roman Emperor in the name of the Roman people. It may be enough to say of one of them, Bolivia, which was recently heard of through her part in the war on the Pacific coast, that out of fourteen Presidents of the Bolivian Republic thirteen have died assassinated or in exile.[6] There is one partial explanation of the inattention of English and European politicians to a most striking, instructive, and uniform body of facts: Spanish—though, next to English, it is the most widely diffused language of the civilised world—is little read or spoken in England, France, or Germany. There are, however, other theories to account for the universal and scarcely intermitted political confusion which at times has reigned in all Central and South America, save Chile and the Brazilian Empire. It is said that the people are to a great extent of Indian blood, and that they have been trained in Roman Catholicism. Such arguments would be intelligible if they were used by persons who maintained that a highly special and exceptional political education is essential to the successful practice of popular government; but they proceed from those who believe that there is at least a strong presumption in favour of democratic institutions everywhere. And

---

[6] Arana, *Guerre du Pacifique,* i. 33.

as regards the Roman Catholic Church, it should at least be remembered that, whatever else it may be, it is a great school of equality.

I have now given shortly the actual history of popular government since it was introduced, in its modern shape, into the civilised world. I state the facts, as matter neither for congratulation nor for lamentation, but simply as materials for opinion. It is manifest that, so far as they go, they do little to support the assumption that popular government has an indefinitely long future before it. Experience rather tends to show that it is characterised by great fragility, and that, since its appearance, all forms of government have become more insecure than they were before. The true reason why the extremely accessible facts which I have noticed are so seldom observed and put together is that the enthusiasts for popular government, particularly when it reposes on a wide basis of suffrage, are actuated by much the same spirit as the zealots of Legitimism. They assume their principle to have a sanction antecedent to fact. It is not thought to be in any way invalidated by practical violations of it, which merely constitute so many sins the more against imprescriptible right. The convinced partisans of democracy care little for instances which show democratic governments to be unstable. These are merely isolated triumphs of the principle of evil. But the conclusion of the sober student of history will not be of this kind. He will rather note it as a fact, to be considered in the most serious spirit, that since the century during which the Roman Emperors were at the mercy of the Prætorian soldiery, there has been no such insecurity of government as the world has seen since rulers became delegates of the community.

Is it possible to assign any reasons for this singular modern loss of political equilibrium? I think that it is possible to a certain extent. It may be observed that two separate national sentiments have been acting on Western Europe since the beginning of the present century. To call them by names given to them by those who dislike them, one is Imperialism and the other is Radicalism. They are not in the least purely British forms of opinion, but are coextensive with civilisation. Almost all men in our day are anxious that their country should be respected of all and dependent on none, that it should enjoy greatness and perhaps ascendency; and this passion for national dignity has gone hand in hand with the desire of the many, ever more and more acquiesced in by the few, to have a share of political power under the name of liberty, and to govern by rulers who are their delegates. The two newest and most striking of political creations in Europe, the German Empire, and the Italian Kingdom, are joint products of these forces. But for the first of these coveted objects, Imperial rank, great armies and fleets are indispensable, and it becomes ever more a necessity that the men under arms should be nearly coextensive with the whole of the males in the flower of life. It has yet to be seen how far great armies are consistent with popular government resting on a wide suffrage. No two organisations can be more opposed to one another than an army scientifically disciplined and equipped, and a nation democratically governed. The great military virtue is obedience; the great military sin is slackness in obeying. It is forbidden to decline to carry out orders, even with the clearest conviction of their inexpediency. But the chief democratic right is the right to censure superiors; public opinion, which means censure as well a praise, is the motive force of democratic societies. The maxims of the two systems flatly contradict one another, and the man who would loyally obey both finds his moral constitution cut into two halves. It has been found by recent experience that the more popular the civil institutions, the harder it is to keep the army from meddling with politics. Military insurrections are made by officers, but not before every soldier has discovered that the share of power which belongs to him as a unit in a regiment is more valuable than his fragment of power as a unit in a constituency. Military revolts are of universal occurrence; but far the largest number have occurred in Spain and the Spanish-speaking countries. There have been ingenious explanations of the phenomenon, but the manifest explanation is Habit. An army which has once interfered with politics is under a strong temptation to interfere again. It is a far easier and far more effective way of causing an opinion to prevail than going to a ballot-box, and far more profitable to the leaders. I may add that, violent as is the improbability of military interference in some countries, there is probably no country except the United States in which the army could not control the government, if it were of one mind and if it retained its military material.

Popular governments have been repeatedly overturned by the Army and the Mob in combination; but on the whole the violent destruction of these governments in their more extreme forms has been effected by the army, while in their more moderate shapes they have had the mob for their principal assailant. It is to be observed that in recent times mobs have materially changed both their character and their method of attack. A mob was once a portion of society in a state of dissolution, a collection of people who for the time had broken loose from the ties which bind society together. It may have had a vague preference for some political or religious cause, but the spirit which animated it was mainly one of mischief, or of disorder, or of panic. But mobs have now come more and more to be the organs of definite opinions. Spanish mobs have impartially worn all colours; but the French mob which overthrew the government of the elder Bourbons in 1830, while it had a distinct political object in its wish to defeat the aggressive measures of the King, had a further bias towards Ultra-Radicalism or Republicanism, which showed itself strongly in the insurrectionary movements that followed the accession of Louis Philippe to the throne. The mob, which in 1848 overturned the government of the younger Bourbons, aimed at establishing a Republic, but it had also a leaning to Socialism; and the frightful popular insurrection of June 1848 was entirely Socialistic. At present, whenever in Europe there is a disturbance like those created by the old mobs, it is in the interest of the parties which style themselves Irreconcileable, and which refuse to submit their opinions to the arbitration of any governments, however wide be the popular suffrage on which they are based. But besides their character, mobs have changed their armament. They formerly wrought destruction by the undisciplined force of sheer numbers; but the mob of Paris, the most successful of all mobs, owed its success to the Barricade. It has now lost this advantage; and a generation is coming to maturity, which perhaps will never have learned that the Paris of to-day has been entirely constructed with the view of rendering for ever impossible the old barricade of paving-stones in the narrow streets of the demolished city. Still more recently, however, the mob has obtained new arms. During the last quarter of a century, a great part, perhaps the greatest part, of the inventive faculties of mankind has been given to the arts of destruction; and among the newly discovered modes of putting an end to human life on a large scale, the most effective and terrible is a manipulation of explosive compounds quite unknown till the other day. The bomb of nitro-glycerine and the parcel of dynamite are as characteristic of the new enemies of government as their Irreconcileable opinions.

There can be no more formidable symptom of our time, and none more menacing to popular government, than the growth of Irreconcileable bodies within the mass of the population. Church and State are alike convulsed by them; but, in civil life, Irreconcileables are associations of men who hold political opinions as men once held religious opinions. They cling to their creed with the same intensity of belief, the same immunity from doubt, the same confident expectation of blessedness to come quickly, which characterises the disciples of an infant faith. They are doubtless a product of democratic sentiment; they have borrowed from it its promise of a new and good time at hand, but they insist on the immediate redemption of the pledge, and they utterly refuse to wait until a popular majority gives effect to their opinions. Nor

would the vote of such a majority have the least authority
with them, if it sanctioned any departure from their principles. It is possible, and indeed likely, that if the Russians
voted by universal suffrage to-morrow, they would con-
firm the Imperial authority by enormous majorities; but
not a bomb nor an ounce of dynamite would be spared
to the reigning Emperor by the Nihilists. The Irreconcileables are of course at feud with governments of the older
type, but these governments make no claim to their support; on the other hand, they are a portion of the governing body of democratic commonwealths, and from this
vantage ground they are able to inflict deadly injury on
popular government. There is in reality no closer analogy
than between these infant political creeds and the bellig-
erent religions which are constantly springing up even
now in parts of the world; for instance, that of the Tae-
pings in China. Even in our own country we may observe
that the earliest political Irreconcileables were religious
or semi-religious zealots. Such were both the Independents and the Jacobites. Cromwell, who for many striking
reasons might have been a personage of a much later age,
was an Irreconcileable at the head of an army; and we all
know what he thought of the Parliament which anticipated the democratic assemblies of our day.

Of all modern Irreconcileables, the Nationalists appear
to be the most impracticable, and of all governments,
popular governments seem least likely to cope with them
successfully. Nobody can say exactly what Nationalism
is, and indeed the dangerousness of the theory arises from
its vagueness. It seems full of the seeds of future civil
convulsion. As it is sometimes put, it appears to assume

that men of one particular race suffer injustice if they are
placed under the same political institutions with men of
another race. But Race is quite as ambiguous a term as
Nationality. The earlier philologists had certainly supposed that the branches of mankind speaking languages
of the same stock were somehow connected by blood; but
no scholar now believes that this is more than approxi-
mately true, for conquest, contact, and the ascendency of
a particular literate class, have quite as much to do with
community of language as common descent. Moreover,
several of the communities claiming the benefit of the
new theory are certainly not entitled to it. The Irish are
an extremely mixed race, and it is only by a perversion
of language that the Italians can be called a race at all. The
fact is that any portion of a political society, which has
had a somewhat different history from the rest of the
parts, can take advantage of the theory and claim independence, and can thus threaten the entire society with
dismemberment. Where royal authority survives in any
vigour, it can to a certain extent deal with these demands.
Almost all the civilised States derive their national unity
from common subjection, past or present, to royal power;
the Americans of the United States, for example, are a
nation because they once obeyed a king. Hence too it is
that such a miscellany of races as those which make up
the Austro-Hungarian Monarchy can be held together,
at all events temporarily, by the authority of the Em-
peror-King. But democracies are quite paralysed by the
plea of Nationality. There is no more effective way of
attacking them than by admitting the right of the
majority to govern, but denying that the majority so en-

titled is the particular majority which claims the right.

The difficulties of popular government, which arise from the modern military spirit and from the modern growth of Irreconcileable parties, could not perhaps have been determined without actual experience. But there are other difficulties which might have been divined, because they proceed from the inherent nature of democracy. In stating some of them, I will endeavour to avoid those which are suggested by mere dislike or alarm: those which I propose to specify were in reality noted more than two centuries ago by the powerful intellect of Hobbes, and it will be seen what light is thrown on some political phenomena of our day by his searching analysis.

Political liberty, said Hobbes, is political power. When a man burns to be free, he is not longing for the "desolate freedom of the wild ass"; what he wants is a share of political government. But, in wide democracies, political power is minced into morsels, and each man's portion of it is almost infinitesimally small. One of the first results of this political comminution is described by Mr. Justice Stephen in a work[7] of earlier date than that which I have quoted above. It is that two of the historical watchwords of Democracy exclude one another, and that, where there is political Liberty, there can be no Equality.

> The man who can sweep the greatest number of fragments of political power into one heap will govern the rest. The strongest man in one form or another will always rule. If the government is a military one, the qualities which make a man a great soldier

---

[7] *Liberty, Fraternity, and Equality,* by Sir James Stephen, 1873, p. 239.

will make him a ruler. If the government is a monarchy, the qualities which kings value in counsellors, in administrators, in generals, will give power. In a pure democracy, the ruling men will be the Wire-pullers and their friends; but they will be no more on an equality with the people than soldiers or Ministers of State are on an equality with the subjects of a Monarchy. . . . In some ages, a powerful character, in others cunning, in others power of transacting business, in others eloquence, in others a good hold upon commonplaces and a facility in applying them to practical purposes, will enable a man to climb on his neighbours' shoulders and direct them this way or that; but under all circumstances the rank and file are directed by leaders of one kind or another who get the command of their collective force.

There is no doubt that, in popular governments resting on a wide suffrage, either without an army or having little reason to fear it, the leader, whether or not he be cunning, or eloquent, or well provided with commonplaces, will be the Wire-puller. The process of cutting up political power into petty fragments has in him its most remarkable product. The morsels of power are so small that men, if left to themselves, would not care to employ them. In England, they would be largely sold, if the law permitted it; in the United States they are extensively sold in spite of the law; and in France, and to a less extent in England, the number of "abstentions" shows the small value attributed to votes. But the political *chiffonnier* who collects and utilises the fragments is the Wire-puller. I think, however, that it is too much the habit in this country to describe him as a mere organiser, contriver, and manager. The particular mechanism which he constructs is no doubt of much importance. The form of this mechanism recently erected in this country has a close resemblance to the system of the Wesleyan Methodists; one system, however, exists for the purpose of keeping the spirit of Grace a-flame, the other for maintaining the spirit of Party at a white heat. The Wire-puller is not intelligible unless we take into account one of the strongest forces acting on human nature—Party feeling. Party feeling is probably far more a survival of the primitive combativeness of mankind than a consequence of conscious intellectual differences between man and man. It is essentially the same sentiment which in certain states of society leads to civil, intertribal, or international war; and it is as universal as humanity. It is better studied in its more irrational manifestations than in those to which we are accustomed. It is said that Australian savages will travel half over the Australian continent to take in a fight the side of combatants who wear the same Totem as themselves. Two Irish factions who broke one another's heads over the whole island are said to have orginated in a quarrel about the colour of a cow. In Southern India, a series of dangerous riots are constantly arising through the rivalry of parties who know no more of one another than that some of them belong to the party of the right hand and others to that of the left hand. Once a year, large numbers of English ladies and gentlemen, who have no serious reason for preferring one University to the other, wear dark or light blue colours to signify good wishes for the success of Oxford or Cambridge in a cricket-match or boat-race. Party differences, properly so called, are supposed to indicate intellectual, or moral, or historical preferences; but these go a very little way down into the population, and by the bulk of partisans they are hardly understood and soon forgotten. "Guelf" and "Ghibelline" had once a meaning, but men were under perpetual banishment from their native land for belonging to one or other of these parties long after nobody knew in what the difference consisted. Some men are Tories or Whigs by conviction; but thousands upon thousands of electors vote simply for yellow, blue, or purple, caught at most by the appeals of some popular orator.

It is through this great natural tendency to take sides that the Wire-puller works. Without it he would be powerless. His business is to fan its flame; to keep it constantly acting upon the man who has once declared himself a partisan; to make escape from it difficult and distasteful. His art is that of the Nonconformist preacher, who gave importance to a body of commonplace religionists by persuading them to wear a uniform and take a military title, or of the man who made the success of a Temperance Society by prevailing on its members to wear always and openly a blue ribbon. In the long-run, these contrivances cannot be confined to any one party, and their effects on all parties and their leaders, and on the whole ruling democracy, must be in the highest degree serious and lasting. The first of these effects will be, I think, to make all parties very like one another, and indeed in the end almost indistinguishable, however leaders may quarrel and partisan hate partisan. In the next place, each party will probably become more and more homogeneous; and the opinions it professes, and the policy which is the outcome of those opinions, will less and less reflect the individual mind of any leader, but only the ideas which seem to that mind to be most likely to win favour with the greatest number of supporters. Lastly, the wire-pulling system, when fully developed, will infallibly lead to the constant enlargement of the area of suffrage. What is called universal suffrage has greatly declined in the estimation, not only of philosophers who follow Bentham, but of the *à priori* theorists who assumed that it was the inseparable accompaniment of a Republic, but who found that in practice it was the natural basis of a tyranny. But extensions of the suffrage, though no longer believed to be good in themselves, have now a permanent place in the armoury of parties, and are sure to be a favourite weapon of the Wire-puller. The Athenian statesmen who, worsted in a quarrel of aristocratic cliques, "took the people into partnership," have a close parallel in the modern politicians who introduce household suffrage into towns to "dish" one side, and into counties to "dish" the other.

Let us now suppose the competition of Parties, stimulated to the utmost by the modern contrivances of the Wire-puller, to have produced an electoral system under which every adult male has a vote, and perhaps every adult female. Let us assume that the new machinery has extracted a vote from every one of these electors. How is the result to be expressed? It is, that the average opinion of a great multitude has been obtained, and that this average opinion becomes the basis and standard of all government and law. There is hardly any experience of the way in which such a system would work, except in the eyes of those who believe that history began since their own birth. The universal suffrage of white males in the United States is about fifty years old; that of white and black is less than twenty. The French threw away universal suffrage after the Reign of Terror; it was twice revived in France, that the Napoleonic tyranny might be founded on it; and it was introduced into Germany, that the personal power of Prince Bismarck might be confirmed. But one of the strangest of vulgar ideas is that a very wide suffrage could or would promote progress, new ideas, new discoveries and inventions, new arts of life. Such a suffrage is commonly associated with Radicalism; and no doubt amid its most certain effects would be the extensive destruction of existing institutions; but the chances are that, in the long-run, it would produce a mischievous form of Conservatism, and drug society with a potion compared with which Eldonine would be a salutary draught. For to what end, towards what ideal state, is the process of stamping upon law the average opinion of an entire community directed? The end arrived at is identical with that of the Roman Catholic Church, which attributes a similar sacredness to the average opinion of the Christian world. "Quod semper, quod ubique, quod ab omnibus," was the canon of Vincent of Lerins. "Securus judicat orbis terrarum," were the words which rang in the ears of Newman and produced such marvellous effects on him. But did any one in his senses ever suppose that these were maxims of progress? The principles of legislation at which they point would probably put an end to all social and political activities, and arrest everything which has ever been associated with Liberalism. A moment's reflection will satisfy any competently instructed person that this is not too broad a proposition. Let him turn over in his mind the great epochs of scientific invention and social change during the last two centuries, and consider what would have occurred if universal suffrage had been established at any one of them. Universal suffrage, which to-day excludes Free Trade from the United States, would certainly have prohibited the spinning-jenny and the power-loom. It would certainly have forbidden the threshing-machine. It would have prevented the adoption of the Gregorian Calendar; and it would have restored the Stuarts. It would have proscribed the Roman Catholics with the mob which burned Lord Mansfield's house and library in 1780, and it would have proscribed the Dissenters with the mob which burned Dr. Priestley's house and library in 1791.

There are possibly many persons who, without denying these conclusions in the past, tacitly assume that no such mistakes will be committed in the future, because the community is already too enlightened for them, and will become more enlightened through popular education. But without questioning the advantages of popular education under certain aspects, its manifest tendency is to diffuse popular commonplaces, to fasten them on the mind at the time when it is most easily impressed, and thus to stereotype average opinion. It is of course possible that universal suffrage would not now force on governments the same legislation which it would infallibly have dictated a hundred years ago; but then we are necessarily ignorant what germs of social and material improvement there may be in the womb of time, and how far they may conflict with the popular prejudice which hereafter will be omnipotent. There is in fact just enough evidence to show that even now there is a marked antagonism be-

tween democratic opinion and scientific truth as applied
to human societies. The central seat in all Political Economy was from the first occupied by the theory of Population. This theory has now been generalised by Mr. Darwin and his followers, and, stated as the principle of the
survival of the fittest, it has become the central truth of
all biological science. Yet it is evidently disliked by the
multitude, and thrust into the background by those
whom the multitude permits to lead it. It has long been
intensely unpopular in France and the continent of
Europe; and, among ourselves, proposals for recognising
it through the relief of distress by emigration are visibly
being supplanted by schemes founded on the assumption
that, through legislative experiments on society, a given
space of land may always be made to support in comfort
the population which from historical causes has come to
be settled on it.

It is perhaps hoped that this opposition between democracy and science, which certainly does not promise
much for the longevity of popular government, may be
neutralised by the ascendency of instructed leaders. Possibly the proposition would not be very unsafe, that he
who calls himself a friend of democracy because he believes that it will be always under wise guidance is in
reality, whether he knows it or not, an enemy of democracy. But at all events the signs of our time are not at all
of favourable augury for the future direction of great
multitudes by statesmen wiser than themselves. The relation of political leaders to political followers seems to me
to be undergoing a twofold change. The leaders may be
as able and eloquent as ever, and some of them certainly

appear to have an unprecedentedly "good hold upon commonplaces, and a facility in applying them," but they are manifestly listening nervously at one end of a speaking-tube which receives at its other end the suggestions of a lower intelligence. On the other hand, the followers, who are really the rulers, are manifestly becoming impatient of the hesitations of their nominal chiefs, and the wrangling of their representatives. I am very desirous of keeping aloof from questions disputed between the two great English parties; but it certainly seems to me that all over Continental Europe, and to some extent in the United States, parliamentary debates are becoming ever more formal and perfunctory, they are more and more liable to being peremptorily cut short, and the true springs of policy are more and more limited to clubs and associations deep below the level of the highest education and experience. There is one State or group of States, whose political condition deserves particular attention. This is Switzerland, a country to which the student of politics may always look with advantage for the latest forms and results of democratic experiment. About forty years ago, just when Mr. Grote was giving to the world the earliest volumes of his *History of Greece,* he published *Seven Letters on the Recent Politics of Switzerland,* explaining that his interest in the Swiss Cantons arose from their presenting "a certain analogy nowhere else to be found in Europe" to the ancient Greek States. Now, if Grote had one object more than another at heart in writing his History, it was to show, by the example of the Athenian democracy, that wide popular governments, so far from meriting the reproach of fickleness, are sometimes characterised by the utmost tenacity of attachment, and will follow the counsels of a wise leader, like Pericles, at the cost of any amount of suffering, and may even be led by an unwise leader, like Nicias, to the very verge of destruction. But he had the acuteness to discern in Switzerland the particular democratic institution, which was likely to tempt democracies into dispensing with prudent and independent direction. He speaks with the strongest disapproval of a provision in the Constitution of Lucerne, by which all laws, passed by the Legislative Council, were to be submitted for veto or sanction to the vote of the people throughout the Canton. This was originally a contrivance of the ultra-Catholic party, and was intended to neutralise the opinions of the Catholic Liberals, by bringing to bear on them the average opinion of the whole Cantonal population. A year after Mr. Grote had published his "Seven Letters," the French Revolution of 1848 occurred, and, three years later, the violent overthrow of the democratic institutions established by the French National Assembly was consecrated by the very method of voting which he had condemned, under the name of the Plébiscite. The arguments of the French Liberal party against the Plébiscite, during the twenty years of stern despotism which it entailed upon France, have always appeared to me to be arguments in reality against the very principle of democracy. After the misfortunes of 1870, the Bonapartes and the Plébiscite were alike involved in the deepest unpopularity; but it seems impossible to doubt that Gambetta, by his agitation for the *scrutin de liste,* was attempting to recover as much as he could of the plebiscitary system of voting. Meantime, it has become, in various shapes, one of the most characteristic of Swiss institutions. One article of the Federal Constitution provides that, if fifty thousand Swiss citizens, entitled to vote, demand the revision of the Constitution, the question whether the Constitution be revised shall be put to the vote of the people of Switzerland, "aye" or "no." Another enacts that, on the petition of thirty thousand citizens, every Federal law and every Federal decree, which is not urgent, shall be subject to the *referendum;* that is, it shall be put to the popular vote. These provisions, that when a certain number of voters demand a particular measure, or require a further sanction for a particular enactment, it shall be put to the vote of the whole country, seem to me to have a considerable future before them in democratically governed societies. When Mr. Labouchere told the House of Commons in 1882 that the people were tired of the deluge of debate, and would some day substitute for it the direct consultation of the constituencies, he had more facts to support his opinion than his auditors were perhaps aware of.

Here then we have one great inherent infirmity of popular governments, an infirmity deducible from the principle of Hobbes, that liberty is power cut into fragments. Popular governments can only be worked by a process which incidentally entails the further subdivision of the morsels of political power; and thus the tendency of these governments, as they widen their electoral basis, is towards a dead level of commonplace opinion, which they are forced to adopt as the standard of legislation and policy. The evils likely to be thus produced are rather those vulgarly associated with Ultra-Conservatism than those of Ultra-Radicalism. So far indeed as the human race has experience, it is not by political societies in any way resembling those now called democracies that human improvement has been carried on. History, said Strauss—and, considering his actual part in life, this is perhaps the last opinion which might have been expected from him—History is a sound aristocrat.[8] There may be oligarchies close enough and jealous enough to stifle thought as completely as an Oriental despot who is at the same time the pontiff of a religion; but the progress of mankind has hitherto been effected by the rise and fall of aristocracies, by the formation of one aristocracy within another, or by the succession of one aristocracy to another. There have been so-called democracies, which have rendered services beyond price to civilisation, but they were only peculiar forms of aristocracy.

The short-lived Athenian democracy, under whose shelter art, science, and philosophy shot so wonderfully upwards, was only an aristocracy which rose on the ruins of one much narrower. The splendour which attracted the original genius of the then civilised world to Athens was provided by the severe taxation of a thousand subject cities; and the skilled labourers who worked under Phidias, and who built the Parthenon, were slaves.

The infirmities of popular government, which consist in its occasional wanton destructiveness, have been frequently dwelt upon and require less attention. In the

---

[8] The opinion of Strauss appears to be shared by M. Ernest Renan. It occurs twice in the singular piece which he calls *Caliban*. "Toute civilisation est d'origine aristocratique" (p. 77). "Toute civilisation est l'œuvre des aristocrates" (p. 91).

long-run, the most interesting question which they suggest is, to what social results does the progressive overthrow of existing institutions promise to conduct mankind? I will again quote Mr. Labouchere, who is not the
less instructive because he may perhaps be suspected of
taking a certain malicious pleasure in stating roundly
what many persons who employ the same political
watchwords as himself are reluctant to say in public, and
possibly shrink from admitting to themselves in their
own minds.

> Democrats are told that they are dreamers, and why? Because
> they assert that, if power be placed in the hands of the many,
> the many will exercise it for their own benefit. Is it not a still
> wilder dream to suppose that the many will in future possess
> power, and use it not to secure what they consider to be their
> interests, but to serve those of others? . . . Is it imagined that
> artisans in our great manufacturing towns are so satisfied with
> their present position that they will hurry to the polls, to register
> their votes in favour of a system which divides us socially,
> politically, and economically, into classes, and places them at the
> bottom with hardly a possibility of rising? . . . Is the lot (of the
> agricultural labourer) so happy a one that he will humbly and
> cheerfully affix his cross to the name of the man who tells him
> that it can never be changed for the better? . . . We know that
> artisans and agricultural labourers will approach the considera-
> tion of political and social problems with fresh and vigorous
> minds. . . . For the moment, we demand the equalisation of the
> franchise. . . . Our next demands will be electoral districts,
> cheap elections, payment of members, and abolition of heredi-
> tary legislators. When our demands are complied with, we shall
> be thankful, but we shall not rest. On the contrary, having
> forged an instrument for democratic legislation, we shall use it.[9]

---

[9] *Fortnightly Review,* March 1, 1883.

The persons who charged Mr. Labouchere with dreaming because he thus predicted the probable course, and defined the natural principles, of future democratic legislation, seem to me to have done him much injustice. His forecast of political events is extremely rational; and I cannot but agree with him in thinking it absurd to suppose that, if the hard-toiled and the needy, the artisan and the agricultural labourer, become the depositaries of power, and if they can find agents through whom it becomes possible for them to exercise it, they will not employ it for what they may be led to believe are their own interests. But in an inquiry whether, independently of the alarm or enthusiasm which they excite in certain persons or classes, democratic institutions contain any seed of dissolution or extinction, Mr. Labouchere's speculation becomes most interesting just where it stops. What is to be the nature of the legislation by which the lot of the artisan and of the agricultural labourer is to be not merely altered for the better, but exchanged for whatever station and fortune they may think it possible to confer on themselves by their own supreme authority? Mr. Labouchere's language, in the above passage and in other parts of his paper, like that of many persons who agree with him in the belief that government can indefinitely increase human happiness, undoubtedly suggests the opinion, that the stock of good things in the world is practically unlimited in quantity, that it is (so to speak) contained in a vast storehouse or granary, and that out of this it is now doled in unequal shares and unfair proportions. It is this unfairness and inequality which democratic law will some day correct. Now I am not concerned to deny that, at various times during the history of mankind, narrow oligarchies have kept too much of the wealth of the world to themselves, or that false economical systems have occasionally diminished the total supply of wealth, and, by their indirect operation, have caused it to be irrationally distributed. Yet nothing is more certain, than that the mental picture which enchains the enthusiasts for benevolent democratic government is altogether false, and that, if the mass of mankind were to make an attempt at redividing the common stock of good things, they would resemble, not a number of claimants insisting on the fair division of a fund, but a mutinous crew, feasting on a ship's provisions, gorging themselves on the meat and intoxicating themselves with the liquors, but refusing to navigate the vessel to port. It is among the simplest of economical truths, that far the largest part of the wealth of the world is constantly perishing by consumption, and that, if it be not renewed by perpetual toil and adventure, either the human race, or the particular community making the experiment of resting without being thankful, will be extinguished or brought to the very verge of extinction.

This position, although it depends in part on a truth of which, according to John Stuart Mill,[10] nobody is habitually aware who has not bestowed some thought on the matter, admits of very simple illustration. It used to be a question hotly debated among Economists how it was that countries recovered with such surprising rapidity from the effects of the most destructive and desolating

---

[10] Mill, *Principles of Political Economy,* i. 5. 5.

wars. "An enemy lays waste a country by fire and sword, and destroys or carries away nearly all the movable wealth existing in it, and yet, in a few years after, everything is much as it was before." Mill,[11] following Chalmers, gives the convincing explanation that nothing in such a case has happened which would not have occurred in any circumstances. "What the enemy has destroyed would have been destroyed in a little time by the inhabitants themselves; the wealth which they so rapidly reproduce would have needed to be reproduced and would have been reproduced in any case, and probably in as short an interval." In fact, the fund by which the life of the human race and of each particular society is sustained, is never in a statical condition. It is no more in that condition than is a cloud in the sky, which is perpetually dissolving and perpetually renewing itself. "Everything which is produced is consumed; both what is saved and what is said to be spent; and the former quite as rapidly as the latter. The wealth of mankind is the result of a continuing process, everywhere complex and delicate, and nowhere of such complexity and delicacy as in the British Islands. So long as this process goes on under existing influences, it is not, as we have seen, interrupted by earthquake, flood, or war; and, at each of its steps, the wealth which perishes and revives has a tendency to increase. But if we alter the character or diminish the force of these influences, are we sure that wealth, instead of increasing, will not dwindle and perhaps disappear?" Mill notes an exception to the revival of a country after war.

---

[11] *Ibid.*, i. 5. 7.

It may be depopulated, and if there are not men to carry it on, the process of reproduction will stop. But may it not be arrested by any means short of exterminating the population? An experience, happily now rare in the world, shows that wealth may come very near to perishing through diminished energy in the motives of the men who reproduce it. You may, so to speak, take the heart and spirit out of the labourers to such an extent that they do not care to work. Jeremy Bentham observed about a century ago that the Turkish Government had in his day impoverished some of the richest countries in the world far more by its action on motives than by its positive exactions; and it has always appeared to me that the destruction of the vast wealth accumulated under the Roman Empire, one of the most orderly and efficient of governments, and the decline of Western Europe into the squalor and poverty of the Middle Ages, can only be accounted for on the same principle. The failure of reproduction through relaxation of motives was once an everyday phenomenon in the East; and this explains to students of Oriental history why it is that throughout its course a reputation for statesmanship was always a reputation for financial statesmanship. In the early days of the East India Company, villages "broken by a severe settlement" were constantly calling for the attention of the Government; the assessment on them did not appear to be excessive on English fiscal principles, but it had been heavy enough to press down the motives to labour, so that they could barely recover themselves. The phenomenon, however, is not confined to the East, where no doubt the motives to toil are more easily affected than in Western societies. No later than the end of the last century, large portions of the French peasantry ceased to cultivate their land, and large numbers of French artisans declined to work, in despair at the vast requisitions of the Revolutionary Government during the Reign of Terror; and, as might be expected, the penal law had to be called in to compel their return to their ordinary occupations.[12]

It is perfectly possible, I think, as Mr. Herbert Spencer has shown in a recent admirable volume,[13] to revive even in our day the fiscal tyranny which once left even European populations in doubt whether it was worth while preserving life by thrift and toil. You have only to tempt a portion of the population into temporary idleness by promising them a share in a fictitious hoard lying (as Mill puts it) in an imaginary strong-box which is supposed to contain all human wealth. You have only to take the heart out of those who would willingly labour and save, by taxing them *ad misericordiam* for the most laudable philanthropic objects. For it makes not the smallest difference to the motives of the thrifty and industrious part of mankind whether their fiscal oppressor be an Eastern despot, or a feudal baron, or a democratic legislature, and whether they are taxed for the benefit of a Corporation called Society, or for the advantage of an individual styled King or Lord. Here then is the great question about democratic legislation, when carried to more than a moderate length. How will it affect human motives? What motives will it

---

[12] Taine, *Origines de la France Contemporaine,* tom. iii., "La Révolution." See, as to artisans, p. 75 (note), and as to cultivators, p. 511.
[13] *The Man versus the State,* by Herbert Spencer. London, 1884.

substitute for those now acting on men? The motives, which at present impel mankind to the labour and pain which produce the resuscitation of wealth in ever-increasing quantities, are such as infallibly to entail inequality in the distribution of wealth. They are the springs of action called into activity by the strenuous and never-ending struggle for existence, the beneficent private war which makes one man strive to climb on the shoulders of another and remain there through the law of the survival of the fittest.

These truths are best exemplified in the part of the world to which the superficial thinker would perhaps look for the triumph of the opposite principle. The United States have justly been called the home of the disinherited of the earth; but, if those vanquished under one sky in the struggle for existence had not continued under another the same battle in which they had been once worsted, there would have been no such exploit performed as the cultivation of the vast American territory from end to end and from side to side. There could be no grosser delusion than to suppose this result to have been attained by democratic legislation. It has really been obtained through the sifting out of the strongest by natural selection. The Government of the United States, which I examine in another part of this volume, now rests on universal suffrage, but then it is only a political government. It is a government under which coercive restraint, except in politics, is reduced to a minimum. There has hardly ever before been a community in which the weak have been pushed so pitilessly to the wall, in which those who have succeeded have so uniformly been the

strong, and in which in so short a time there has arisen
so great an inequality of private fortune and domestic
luxury. And at the same time, there has never been a
country in which, on the whole, the persons distanced in
the race have suffered so little from their ill-success. All
this beneficent prosperity is the fruit of recognising the
principle of population, and the one remedy for its excess
in perpetual emigration. It all reposes on the sacredness
of contract and the stability of private property, the first
the implement, and the last the reward, of success in the
universal competition. These, however, are all principles
and institutions which the British friends of the "artisan"
and "agricultural labourer" seem not a little inclined to
treat as their ancestors did agricultural and industrial machinery. The Americans are still of opinion that more is
to be got for human happiness by private energy than by
public legislation. The Irish, however, even in the United
States, are of another opinion, and the Irish opinion is
manifestly rising into favour here. But on the question,
whether future democratic legislation will follow the new
opinion, the prospects of popular government to a great
extent depend. There are two sets of motives, and two
only, by which the great bulk of the materials of human
subsistence and comfort have hitherto been produced and
reproduced. One has led to the cultivation of the territory
of the Northern States of the American Union, from the
Atlantic to the Pacific. The other had a considerable share
in bringing about the industrial and agricultural progress
of the Southern States, and in old days it produced the
wonderful prosperity of Peru under the Incas. One system is economical competition; the other consists in the

daily task, perhaps fairly and kindly allotted, but enforced by the prison or the scourge. So far as we have any experience to teach us, we are driven to the conclusion, that every society of men must adopt one system or the other, or it will pass through penury to starvation.

I have thus shown that popular governments of the modern type have not hitherto proved stable as compared with other forms of political rule, and that they include certain sources of weakness which do not promise security for them in the near or remote future. My chief conclusion can only be stated negatively. There is not at present sufficient evidence to warrant the common belief, that these governments are likely to be of indefinitely long duration. There is, however, one positive conclusion from which no one can escape who bases a forecast of the prospects of popular government, not on moral preference or *à priori* assumption, but on actual experience as witnessed to by history. If there be any reason for thinking that constitutional freedom will last, it is a reason furnished by a particular set of facts, with which Englishmen ought to be familiar, but of which many of them, under the empire of prevailing ideas, are exceedingly apt to miss the significance. The British Constitution has existed for a considerable length of time, and therefore free institutions generally may continue to exist. I am quite aware that this will seem to some a commonplace conclusion, perhaps as commonplace as the conclusion of M. Taine, who, after describing the conquest of all France by the Jacobin Club, declares that his inference is so simple, that he hardly ventures to state it. "Jusqu'à présent, je n'ai guère trouvé qu'un (principe) si simple qu'il semblera puéril et que j'ose à peine l'énoncer. Il consiste tout entier dans cette remarque, qu'une société humaine, surtout une société moderne, est une chose vaste et compliquée." This observation, that "a human society, and particularly a modern society, is a vast and complicated thing," is in fact the very proposition which Burke enforced with all the splendour of his eloquence and all the power of his argument; but, as M. Taine says, it may now seem to some too simple and commonplace to be worth putting into words. In the same way, many persons in whom familiarity has bred contempt, may think it a trivial observation that the British Constitution, if not (as some call it) a holy thing, is a thing unique and remarkable. A series of undesigned changes brought it to such a condition, that satisfaction and impatience, the two great sources of political conduct, were both reasonably gratified under it. In this condition it became, not metaphorically but literally, the envy of the world, and the world took on all sides to copying it. The imitations have not been generally happy. One nation alone, consisting of Englishmen, has practised a modification of it successfully, amidst abounding material plenty. It is not too much to say, that the only evidence worth mentioning for the duration of popular government is to be found in the success of the British Constitution during two centuries under special conditions, and in the success of the American Constitution during one century under conditions still more peculiar and more unlikely to recur. Yet, so far as our own Constitution is concerned, that nice balance of attractions, which caused it to move evenly on its stately path, is perhaps destined to be disturbed. One of the forces governing it may gain dangerously at the expense of the other; and the British political system, with the national greatness and material prosperity attendant on it, may yet be launched into space and find its last affinities in silence and cold.

ESSAY II

THE NATURE OF DEMOCRACY

John Austin, a name honoured in the annals of English jurisprudence, published shortly before his death a pamphlet called *A Plea for the Constitution*. In this publication,[1] which marks the farthest rebound of a powerful mind from the peculiar philosophical Radicalism of the immediate pupils of Jeremy Bentham, Austin applies the analytical power, on which his fame rests, to a number of expressions which entered in his day, as they do in ours, into every political discussion. Among them, he examines the terms Aristocracy and Democracy, and of the latter he says:

> Democracy is still more ambiguous than Aristocracy. It signifies properly a form of government, that is, any government in which the governing body is a comparatively large fraction of the entire nation. As used loosely, and particularly by French writers, it signifies the body of the nation, or the lower part of

---

[1] *A Plea for the Constitution*, by John Austin. London, 1859.

the nation, or a way of thinking and feeling favourable to demo-
cratical government. It not unfrequently bears the meaning
which is often given to the word "people," or the words "sovereign people," that is, some large portion of the nation which is
not actually sovereign, but to which, in the opinion of the
speaker, the sovereignty ought to be transferred.

The same definition of Democracy, in its only proper
and consistent sense, is given by M. Edmond Scherer, in
his powerful and widely circulated pamphlet, named *La
Démocratie et la France.*[2] I shall have to refer presently to M.
Scherer's account of the methods by which the existing
French political system is made to discharge the duties of
government; but, meantime, the greatest merit of his
publication does not seem to me to lie in its exposure of
the servility of the deputies to the electoral committees,
or of the public extravagance by which their support is
purchased. It lies rather in M. Scherer's examination of
certain vague abstract propositions, which are commonly
accepted without question by the Republican politicians
of France, and indeed of the whole Continent. In our day,
when the extension of popular government is throwing
all the older political ideas into utter confusion, a man of
ability can hardly render a higher service to his country,
than by the analysis and correction of the assumptions
which pass from mind to mind in the multitude, without
inspiring a doubt of their truth and genuineness. Some
part of this intellectual circulating medium was base from
the first; another was once good coin, but it is clipped and
worn on all sides; another consists of mere tokens, which

---

[2] *La Démocratie et la France.* Études par Edmond Scherer. Paris, 1883.

are called by an old name, because there is a conventional
understanding that it shall still be used. It is urgently
necessary to rate all this currency at its true value; and,
as regards a part of it, this was done once for all by Sir
J. F. Stephen, in his admirable volume on *Liberty, Fraternity,
and Equality.* But the political smashers are constantly at
work, and their dupes are perpetually multiplying, while
there is by no means a corresponding activity in applying
the proper tests to all this spurious manufacture. We Englishmen pass on the Continent as masters of the art of
government; yet it may be doubted whether, even among
us, the science, which corresponds to the art, is not very
much in the condition of Political Economy before Adam
Smith took it in hand. In France the condition of political
thought is even worse. Englishmen abandon a political
dogma when it has led to practical disaster. But it has
been the lot of Frenchmen to have their attention fastened on the last eleven years of the last century and on
the first fifteen of the present, almost to the exclusion of
the rest of their history; and the political ideas which
grew up during this period have hardly relaxed their hold
on the French intellect at all, after seventy years of further
experience.

   M. Scherer, so far as my knowledge extends, has been
the first French writer to bring into clear light the simple
truth stated by Austin, that Democracy means properly
a particular form of government.[3] This truth, in modern
Continental politics, is the beginning of wisdom. There
is no word about which a denser mist of vague language,

---

[3] Scherer, p. 3.

and a larger heap of loose metaphors, has collected. Yet, although Democracy does signify something indeterminate, there is nothing vague about it. It is simply and solely a form of government. It is the government of the State by the Many, as opposed, according to the old Greek analysis, to its government by the Few, and to its government by One. The border between the Few and the Many, and again between the varieties of the Many, is necessarily indeterminate; but Democracy not the less remains a mere form of government; and, inasmuch as of these forms the most definite and determinate is Monarchy—the government of the State by one person— Democracy is most accurately described as inverted Monarchy. And this description answers to the actual historical process by which the great modern Republics have been formed. Villari[4] has shown that the modern State of the Continental type, with distinctly defined administrative departments as its organs, was first constituted in Italy. It grew, not out of the mediæval Republican municipalities, which had nothing in common with modern governments, but out of that most ill-famed of all political systems, the Italian tyranny or Princedom. The celebrated Italian state-craft, spread all over Europe by Italian statesmen, who were generally ecclesiastics, was applied to France by Louis XIV and Colbert, the pupils of Cardinal Mazarin; and out of the contact of this new science with an administrative system in complete disorder, there sprang Monarchical France. The successive French Republics have been nothing but the later

---

[4] Villari, *Machiavelli,* i. 15, 36, 37.

French Monarchy, upside down. Similarly, the Constitutions and the legal systems of the several North American States, and of the United States, would be wholly unintelligible to anybody who did not know that the ancestors of the Anglo-Americans had once lived under a King, himself the representative of older Kings infinitely more autocratic, and who had not observed that throughout these bodies of law and plans of government the People had simply been put into the King's seat, occasionally filling it with some awkwardness. The advanced Radical politician of our day would seem to have an impression that Democracy differs from Monarchy in essence. There can be no grosser mistake than this, and none more fertile of further delusions. Democracy, the government of the commonwealth by a numerous but indeterminate portion of the community taking the place of the Monarch, has exactly the same conditions to satisfy as Monarchy; it has the same functions to discharge, though it discharges them through different organs. The tests of success in the performance of the necessary and natural duties of a government are precisely the same in both cases.

Thus in the very first place, Democracy, like Monarchy, like Aristocracy, like any other government, must preserve the national existence. The first necessity of a State is that it should be durable. Among mankind regarded as assemblages of individuals, the gods are said to love those who die young; but nobody has ventured to make such an assertion of States. The prayers of nations to Heaven have been, from the earliest ages, for long national life, life from generation to generation, life prolonged far beyond that of children's children, life like that of the everlasting hills. The historian will sometimes speak of governments distinguished for the loftiness of their aims, and the brilliancy of the talents which they called forth, but doomed to an existence all too brief. The compliment is in reality a paradox, for in matters of government all objects are vain and all talents wasted, when they fail to secure national durability. One might as well eulogise a physician for the assiduity of his attendance and the scientific beauty of his treatment, when the patient has died under his care. Next perhaps to the paramount duty of maintaining national existence, comes the obligation incumbent on Democracies, as on all governments, of securing the national greatness and dignity. Loss of territory, loss of authority, loss of general respect, loss of self-respect, may be unavoidable evils, but they are terrible evils, judged by the pains they inflict and the elevation of the minds by which these pains are felt; and the Government which fails to provide a sufficient supply of generals and statesmen, of soldiers and administrators, for the prevention and cure of these evils, is a government which has miscarried. It will also have miscarried, if it cannot command certain qualities which are essential to the success of national action. In all their relations with one another (and this is a fundamental assumption of International law) States must act as individual men. The defects which are defects in individual men, and perhaps venial defects, are faults in States, and generally faults of the extremest gravity. In all war and all diplomacy, in every part of foreign policy, caprice, wilfulness, loss of self-command, timidity, temerity, inconsistency, indecency, and coarseness, are weaknesses which rise to the

level of destructive vices; and if Democracy is more liable
to them than are other forms of government, it is to that
extent inferior to them. It is better for a nation, according
to an English prelate, to be free than to be sober. If the
choice has to be made, and if there is any real connection
between Democracy and liberty, it is better to remain a
nation capable of displaying the virtues of a nation than
even to be free.

  If we turn from the foreign to the domestic duties of
a nation, we shall find the greatest of them to be, that its
government should compel obedience to the law, criminal
and civil. The vulgar impression no doubt is, that laws
enforce themselves. Some communities are supposed to
be naturally law-abiding, and some are not. But the truth
is (and this is a commonplace of the modern jurist) that
it is always the State which causes laws to be obeyed. It
is quite true that this obedience is rendered by the great
bulk of all civilised societies without an effort and quite
unconsciously. But that is only because, in the course of
countless ages, the stern discharge of their chief duty by
States has created habits and sentiments which save the
necessity for penal interference, because nearly everybody shares them. The venerable legal formulas, which
make laws to be administered in the name of the King,
formulas which modern Republics have borrowed, are a
monument of the grandest service which governments
have rendered, and continue to render, to mankind. If any
government should be tempted to neglect, even for a
moment, its function of compelling obedience to law—if
a Democracy, for example, were to allow a portion of the
multitude of which it consists to set some law at defiance

which it happens to dislike—it would be guilty of a crime which hardly any other virtue could redeem, and which century upon century might fail to repair.

On the whole, the dispassionate student of politics, who has once got into his head that Democracy is only a form of government, who has some idea of what the primary duties of government are, and who sees the main question, in choosing between them, to be which of them in the long-run best discharges these duties, has a right to be somewhat surprised at the feelings which the advent of Democracy excites. The problem which this event, if it be near at hand, suggests, is not sentimental but practical; and one might have expected less malediction on one side, and less shouting and throwing up of caps on the other. The fact, however, is that, when the current of human political tastes, which in the long course of ages has been running in all sorts of directions, sets strongly towards one particular point, there is always an outburst of terror or enthusiasm; and the explanation of the feelings roused on such occasions, which is true for our day and of a tendency towards Democracy, is probably true also for all time. The great virtue of Democracies in some men's eyes, their great vice in the eyes of others, is that they are thought to be more active than other forms of government in the discharge of one particular function. This is the alteration and transformation of law and custom—the process known to us as reforming legislation. As a matter of fact, this process—which is an indispensable, though in the long-run a very subordinate, province of a good modern government—is not at all peculiar to Democracies. If the whole of the known his-

tory of the human race be examined, we shall see that the
great authors of legislative change have been powerful
Monarchies. The long wail at the iniquities of Nineveh
and Babylon, which runs through the latter part of the
Old Testament, is the expression of Jewish resentment at
the "big legislation" with which the nations that most
study the Old Testament are supposed to have fallen in
love. The trituration of old usage was carried infinitely
further by the Roman Emperors, ever increasing in thor-
oughness as the despotism grew more stringent. The Emperor was in fact the symbolic beast which the Prophet
saw devouring, breaking to pieces and stamping the residue with its feet. We ourselves live in the dust of Roman
Imperialism, and by far the largest part of modern law is
nothing more than a sedimentary formation left by the
Roman legal reforms. The rule holds good through all
subsequent history. The one wholesale legal reformer of
the Middle Ages was Charles the Great. It was the French
Empire of the Bonapartes that gave real practical currency
to the new French jurisprudence which has overrun the
civilised world, for the governments immediately arising
out of the Revolution left little behind them beyond
projects of law or laws which were practically inapplica-
ble from the contradictions which they contained.

The truth seems to be that the extreme forms of government, Monarchy and Democracy, have a peculiarity
which is absent from the more tempered political systems
founded on compromise, Constitutional Kingship and
Aristocracy. When they are first established in absolute
completeness, they are highly destructive. There is a general, sometimes chaotic, upheaval, while the *nouvelles*

couches are settling into their place in the transformed commonwealth. The new rulers sternly insist, that everything shall be brought into strict conformity with the central principle of the system over which they preside; and they are aided by numbers of persons to whom the old principles were hateful, from their fancy for ideal reforms, from impatience of a monotonous stability, or from a natural destructiveness of temperament. What the old monarchies, established in the valleys of the great Eastern rivers, had to contend against was religious tenacity and tribal obstinacy; and they transported whole populations in order that these might be destroyed. What a modern Democracy fights with is privilege; and it knows no rest till this is trampled out. But the legislation of absolutism, democratic or otherwise, is transitory. Before the Jews had taken home their harps from Babylon, they found themselves the subjects of another mighty conquering Monarchy, of which they observed with wonder that the law of the Medes and Persians altereth not. There is no belief less warranted by actual experience, than that a democratic republic is, after the first and in the long-run, given to reforming legislation. As is well known to scholars, the ancient republics hardly legislated at all; their democratic energy was expended upon war, diplomacy, and justice; but they put nearly insuperable obstacles in the way of a change of law. The Americans of the United States have hedged themselves round in exactly the same way. They only make laws within the limits of their Constitutions, and especially of the Federal Constitution; and, judged by what has become the English standard, their legislation within these limits is almost trivial. As I attempted to show in my first essay, the legislative infertility of democracies springs from permanent causes. The prejudices of the people are far stronger than those of the privileged classes; they are far more vulgar; and they are far more dangerous, because they are apt to run counter to scientific conclusions. This assertion is curiously confirmed by the political phenomena of the moment. The most recent of democratic inventions is the "Referendum" of the Swiss Federal Constitution, and of certain Cantonal Constitutions. On the demand of a certain number of citizens, a law voted by the Legislature is put to the vote of the entire population, lest by any chance its "mandate" should have been exceeded. But to the confusion and dismay of the Radical leaders in the Legislature, the measures which they most prized, when so put, have been negatived.

Democracy being what it is, the language used of it in our day, under its various disguises of Freedom, the "Revolution," the "Republic," Popular Government, the Reign of the People, is exceedingly remarkable. Every sort of metaphor, signifying irresistible force, and conveying admiration or dread, has been applied to it by its friends or its enemies. A great English orator once compared it to the Grave, which takes everything and gives nothing back. The most widely read American historian altogether loses himself in figures of speech. "The change which Divine wisdom ordained, and which no human policy or force could hold back, proceeded as uniformly and majestically as the laws of being, and was as certain as the decrees of eternity."[5] And again, "The idea of freedom had never been wholly unknown; . . . the rising light flashed joy across the darkest centuries, and its growing energy can be traced in the tendency of the ages."[6] These hopes have even found room for themselves among the commonplaces of after-dinner oratory. "The great tide of Democracy is rolling on, and no hand can stay its majestic course," said Sir Wilfrid Lawson of the Franchise Bill.[7] But the strongest evidence of the state of excitement into which some minds are thrown by an experiment in government, which is very old and has never been particularly successful, is afforded by a little volume with the title *Towards Democracy*. The writer is not destitute of poetical force, but the smallest conception of what Democracy really is makes his rhapsodies about it astonishing. "Freedom!" sings this disciple of Walt Whitman—

> And among the far nations there is a stir like the stir of the leaves of the forest.
> Joy, joy, arising on earth.
> And lo! the banners lifted from point to point, and the spirits of the ancient races looking abroad—the divinely beautiful daughters of God calling to their children.
>
> .   .   .   .   .   .

---

[5] Bancroft, *History of the United States*, "The American Revolution," vol. i., p. 1. Mr. Bancroft was almost verbally anticipated in this sentence by a person whom he resembles in nothing except in his love of phrases. "Français républicains," said Maximilien Robespierre, in his speech at the festival of the Supreme Being, "n'est-ce pas l'Être Suprême qui, dès le commencement des temps, décréta la République?"

[6] Bancroft, *ubi supra*, p. 2.

[7] On April 15, 1884.

Lo! the divine East from ages and ages back intact her priceless jewel of thought—the germ of Democracy—bringing down!

.   .   .   .   .   .

O glancing eyes! O leaping shining waters! Do I not know that thou, Democracy, dost control and inspire; that thou too hast relations to them,
As surely as Niagara has relations to Erie and Ontario?

Towards the close of the poem this line occurs—"I heard a voice say, What is Freedom?" It is impossible that the voice could ask a more pertinent question. If the author of *Towards Democracy* had ever heard the answer of Hobbes, that Freedom is "political power divided into small fragments," or the dictum of John Austin and M. Scherer, that "Democracy is a form of government," his poetical vein might have been drowned, but his mind would have been invigorated by the healthful douche of cold water.

The opinion that Democracy was irresistible and inevitable, and probably perpetual, would, only a century ago, have appeared a wild paradox. There had been more than 2,000 years of tolerably well-ascertained political history, and at its outset, Monarchy, Aristocracy, and Democracy, were all plainly discernible. The result of a long experience was, that some Monarchies and some Aristocracies had shown themselves extremely tenacious of life. The French monarchy and the Venetian oligarchy were in particular of great antiquity, and the Roman empire was not even then quite dead. But the democracies which had risen and perished, or had fallen into extreme insignificance, seemed to show that this form of government was of rare occurrence in political history, and was characterised by an extreme fragility. This was the opinion of the fathers of the American Federal Republic, who over and over again betray their regret that the only government which it was possible for them to establish was one which promised so little stability. It became very shortly the opinion of the French Revolutionists, for no sooner has the Constitutional Monarchy fallen than the belief that a new era has begun for the human race gives signs of rapidly fading; and the language of the Revolutionary writers becomes stained with a dark and ever-growing suspiciousness, manifestly inspired by genuine fear that Democracy must perish, unless saved by unflagging energy and unsparing severity. Nevertheless, the view that Democracy is irresistible is of French origin, like almost all other sweeping political generalisations. It may be first detected about fifty years ago, and it was mainly spread over the world by the book of De Tocqueville on Democracy in America. Some of the younger speculative minds in France were deeply struck by the revival of democratic ideas in France at the Revolution of 1830, and among them was Alexis de Tocqueville, born a noble and educated in Legitimism. The whole fabric of French Revolutionary belief had apparently been ruined beyond hope of recovery, ruined by the crimes and usurpations of the Convention, by military habits and ideas, by the tyranny of Napoleon Bonaparte, by the return of the Bourbons with a large part of the system of the older monarchy, by the hard repression of the Holy Alliance. Yet so slight a provocation as the attempt of Charles X to do what his brother had done[8] without serious resist-

---

[8] By his Ordinance of September 1816.

ance, brought back the whole torrent of revolutionary
sentiment and dogma, which at once overran the entire
European continent. No doubt it seemed as if there were
something in Democracy which made it resistless; and
yet, as M. Scherer has shown in one of the most valuable
parts of his pamphlet, the Frenchmen of that idea did not
mean the same thing as the modern French Extremist or
the English Radical when they spoke of Democracy. If
their view be put affirmatively, they meant the ascendency of the middle classes; if negatively, they meant the
non-revival of the old feudal society. The French people
were very long in shaking off their fear that the material
advantages, secured to them by the first French Revolution, were not safe; and this fear it was which, as we
perceive from the letters of Mallet du Pan,[9] reconciled
them to the tyranny of the Jacobins and caused them to
look with the deepest suspicion on the plans of the Sovereigns allied against the Republic. Democracy, however,
gradually took a new sense, chiefly under the influence
of wonder at the success of the American Federation, in
which most of the States had now adopted universal suffrage; and by 1848 the word had come to be used very
much with its ancient meaning, the government of the
commonwealth by the Many. It is perhaps the scientific

---

[9] The newly published correspondence of Mallet du Pan with the Court of
Vienna, between 1794 and 1798, is of the highest interest and value. M.
Taine, who contributes the Preface, has several times affirmed that Mallet
was one of the very few persons who understood the French Revolution.
It seems clear that, while these letters were being written, the Republic was
falling into the deepest unpopularity, mitigated only by the fears of which
we have spoken above. It was undoubtedly saved by the military genius of
Napoleon Bonaparte. The one serious mistake of Mallet was his blindness
to that genius. He thought General Bonaparte a charlatan.

tinge which thought is assuming among us that causes so many Englishmen to take for granted that Democracy is inevitable, because many considerable approaches to it have been made in our country. No doubt, if adequate causes are at work, the effect will always follow; but, in politics, the most powerful of all causes are the timidity, the listlessness, and the superficiality, of the generality of minds. If a large number of Englishmen, belonging to classes which are powerful if they exert themselves, continue saying to themselves and others that Democracy is irresistible and must come, beyond all doubt it will come.

The enthusiasm for Democracy, which is conveyed by the figures of speech applied to it, is equally modern with the impression of its inevitableness. In reality, considering the brilliant stages in the history of a certain number of commonwealths with which Democracy has been associated, nothing is more remarkable than the small amount of respect for it professed by actual observers, who had the opportunity and the capacity for forming a judgment on it. Mr. Grote did his best to explain away the poor opinion of the Athenian Democracy entertained by the philosophers who filled the schools of Athens; but the fact remains that the founders of political philosophy found themselves in presence of Democracy, in its pristine vigour, and thought it a bad form of government. The panegyrics of which it is now the object are, again, of French origin. They come to us from the oratory and literature of the first French Revolution, which, however, soon exchanged glorification of the new birth of the human race for a strain of gloomy suspicion and homicidal denunciation. The language of admiration which pre-

vailed for a while had still remoter sources; and it may
be observed, as an odd circumstance, that, while the
Jacobins generally borrowed their phraseology from the
legendary history of the early Roman Republic, the Girondins preferred resorting for metaphors to the literature
which sprang from Rousseau. On the whole, I think that
the historical ignorance which made heroes of Brutus and
Scævola was less abjectly nonsensical than the philosophical silliness which dwelt on the virtues of mankind
in a state of natural democracy. If anybody wishes to
know what was the influence of Rousseau in diffusing the
belief in a golden age, when men lived, like brothers, in
freedom and equality, he should read, not so much the
writings of the sage, as the countless essays printed in
France by his disciples just before 1789. They furnish
very disagreeable proof that the intellectual flower of a
cultivated nation may be brought, by fanatical admiration of a social and political theory, into a condition of
downright mental imbecility.[10] The language of the
Jacobins and the language of the Girondins might be
thought to have perished amid ridicule and disgust; but,
in fact, it underwent a rehabilitation, like that which has
fallen to the lot of Catiline, of Nero, and of Richard III.

---

[10] Brissot, the Girondin leader, while still a young man and an enthusiastic
Royalist, had argued, long before Proudhon, that Property is Theft. There
is, he said, a natural right to correct the injustice of the institution, by
stealing. But he held the still more remarkable opinion, that cannibalism is
natural and justifiable. Since, he argued, under the reign of Nature the sheep
does not spare the insects on the grass, and the wolf and the man eat the
sheep, why have not all these creatures a natural right to eat creatures of
their own kind? *(Recherches philosophiques sur le droit de propriété et sur le vol considéré
dans sa nature.* Par Brissot de Warville.)

Tocqueville thought Democracy was inevitable, but he looked on its approach with distrust and dread. In the course, however, of the succeeding fifteen years two books were published, which, whatever their popularity, might fairly be compared with the writings of which we have spoken above, for a total abnegation of common sense. Louis Blanc[11] took the homicidal pedant, Robespierre, for his hero; Lamartine, the feeble and ephemeral sect of Girondins; and from the works of these two writers has proceeded much the largest part of the language eulogistic of Democracy, which pervades the humbler political literature of the Continent, and now of Great Britain also.

There is indeed one kind of praise which Democracy has received, and continues to receive, in the greatest abundance. This is praise addressed to the governing Demos by those who fear it, or desire to conciliate it, or hope to use it. When it has once become clear that Democracy is a form of government, it will be easily understood what panegyrics of the multitude amount to. Democracy is Monarchy inverted, and the modes of addressing the multitude are the same as the modes of addressing kings. The more powerful and jealous the sovereign, the more unbounded is the eulogy, the more extravagant is the tribute. "O King, live for ever," was the ordinary formula of beginning an address to the

---

[11] The *Histoire des Girondins* of Lamartine was published in 1847. The publication of the *Histoire de la Révolution Française* of Louis Blanc began in 1847, and went on till 1862; the *Histoire de Dix Ans* of the same writer had been published in 1841–44. The first part of De Tocqueville's work was published in 1835, the second in 1839.

Babylonian or Median king, drunk or sober. "Your ascent to power proceeded as uniformly and majestically as the laws of being and was as certain as the decrees of eternity," says Mr. Bancroft to the American people. Such flattery proceeds frequently from the ignobler parts of human nature, but not always. What seems to us baseness, passed two hundred years ago at Versailles for gentleness and courtliness; and many people have every day before them a monument of what was once thought suitable language to use of a King of England, in the Dedication of the English Bible to James I. There is no reason to suppose that this generation will feel any particular shame at flattery, though the flattery will be addressed to the people and not to the King. It may even become commoner, through the growth of scientific modes of thought. Dean Church, in his recent volume on "Bacon," has made his original remark that Bacon behaved himself to powerful men as he behaved himself to Nature. *Parendo vinces.* If you resist Nature, she will crush you; but if you humour her, she will place her tremendous forces at your disposal. It is madness to offer direct resistance to a royal virago or a royal pedant, but by subservience you may command either of them. There is much of this feeling in the state of mind of intelligent and highly educated Radicals, when they are in presence of a mob. They make their choice, according to the composition of their audience, between two wonderful alternative theories of our day—one, that the artisan of the towns knows everything, because his work is so monotonous, and because he has so much time on his hands; the other, that the labourer of the country districts knows everything, because his work is so various and his faculties so constantly active through this variety. Thus it comes to pass that an audience composed of roughs or clowns is boldly told by an educated man that it has more political information than an equal number of scholars. This is not the opinion of the speaker; but it may be made, he thinks, the opinion of the mob, and he knows that the mob could not act as if it were true, unless it worked through scholarly instruments.

The best safeguard against the various delusions and extravagances which I have been examining is a little better knowledge of the true lines of movement which the political affairs of mankind have followed. In the opinion of a number of English gentlemen, whose authority is now somewhat on the decline, political history began in 1688. Mr. Bright seems to me to express himself often as if he thought that it began with the commencement of the Anti-Corn-Law agitation, and might be considered as having been practically arrested when the Corn-Law was repealed in 1846. There are younger men who are persuaded that it commenced with a certain crisis in the municipal history of Birmingham. The truth, however, is, that we live in a day in which a strand is unwinding itself, which was steadily knitting itself up during long ages. It is difficult to imagine a more baseless historical generalisation than that which Mr. Bancroft addresses to his American readers. During all the period when a change was proceeding "which no human policy could hold back," the movement of political affairs—what Mr. Bancroft calls the "tendency of the ages"—was as distinctly towards Monarchy as it now is towards Democracy. Mankind appear to have begun that stage in their history, which is more or less visible to our eyes, with the germs in each society of all the three definite forms of government—Monarchy, Aristocracy, and Democracy. Everywhere the King and Popular Assembly are seen side by side, the first a priestly and judicial, but primarily a fighting, personage; the last sometimes under the control of an aristocratic Senate, and itself varying from a small oligarchy to something like the entirety of the free male population. At the dawn of history, Aristocracy seems to be gaining on Monarchy, and Democracy on Aristocracy. And this passage of political development is especially well known to us through the accidents which have preserved to us a portion of the records of two famous societies, the Athenian Republic, the cradle of philosophy and art, and the Roman Republic, which began the conquests destined to embrace a great part of the world. This last Republic was always more or less of an Aristocracy; but from the time of its fall, and the establishment of the Roman Empire, there was on the whole, for seventeen centuries, an all but universal movement towards kingship. There were, no doubt, evanescent revivals of popular government. The barbarian races, when they broke into the central Roman territory, brought with them very generally some amount of the ancient tribal liberty which, reintroduced into Mediterranean Europe, seemed again for a while likely to prove the seed of political freedom. The Roman municipal system, left to work unchecked within the walled cities of Northern Italy, reproduced a form of democracy. But Italian Commonwealths, and feudal Estates and Parliaments, all sank, with one memorable exception, before the ever-growing power and prestige of military despotic governments. The historian of our day is apt to moralise and lament over the change, but it was everywhere in the highest degree popular, and it called forth an enthusiasm quite as genuine as that of the modern Radical for the coming Democracy. The Roman Empire, the Italian tyrannies, the English Tudor Monarchy, the French centralised Kingship, the Napoleonic despotism, were all hailed with acclamation, most of it perfectly sincere, either because anarchy had been subdued, or because petty local and domestic oppressions were kept under, or because new energy was infused into national policy. In our own country, the popular government, born of tribal freedom, revived sooner than elsewhere; protected by the insularity of its home, it managed to live; and thus the British Constitution became the one important exception to the "tendency of the ages," and through its remote influence this tendency was reversed, and the movement to Democracy began again. Nevertheless, even with us, though the King might be feared or disliked, the King's office never lost its popularity. The Commonwealth and the Protectorate were never for a moment in real favour with the nation. The true enthusiasm was reserved for the Restoration. Thus, from the reign of Augustus Cæsar to the establishment of the United States, it was Democracy which was always, as a rule, on the decline, nor was the decline arrested till the American Federal Government was founded, itself the offspring of the British Constitution. At this moment, Democracy is receiving the same unqualified eulogy which was once poured on Monarchy;

and though in its modern shape it is the product of a whole series of accidents, it is regarded by some as propelled in a continuous progress by an irresistible force.

Independently of the historical question, how the fashion of bowing profoundly before Democracy grew up, it has to be considered how far the inverted Monarchy, which bears this name, deserves the reverence paid to it. The great philosophical writer who had the best opinion of it was Jeremy Bentham. His authority had to do with the broad extension of the suffrage in most of the States of the American Union, and he was the intellectual father of the masculine school of English Radicals which died out with Mr. Grote. He claimed for governments having the essential characteristics of Democracy, that they were much more free than other governments from what he called "sinister" influences. He meant by a sinister influence, a motive leading a government to prefer the interest of small portions of a community to the interest of the whole. I certainly think that, with an all-important qualification to be mentioned presently, this credit was justly claimed for Democracy by Bentham, and with especial justice in relation to the circumstances of his own time. During the most active period of his long life the French Revolution had stopped all progress, and amid the relaxation of public watchfulness which followed, all sorts of small interests had found themselves niches in the English Budget, like the robber barons of mediæval Italy and Germany on every precipitous hill. Bentham thought it natural that they should do this. The lords of life, he said, are pleasure and pain. Every man follows his own interest as he understands it, and the part of the community which has political power will use it for its own objects. The remedy is to transfer political power to the entire community. It is impossible that they should abuse it, for the interest which they will try to promote is the interest of all, and the interest of all is the proper end and object of all legislation.

On this apparently irresistible reasoning, one or two remarks have to be made. In the first place, the praise here claimed for Democracy is shared by it with Monarchy, particularly in its most absolute forms. There is no doubt that the Roman Emperor cared more for the general good of the vast group of societies subject to him, than the aristocratic Roman Republic had done. The popularity of the great kings who broke up European feudalism, arose from their showing to all their vassals a far more even impartiality than could be obtained from petty feudal rulers; and in our own day, vague and shadowy as are the recommendations of what is called a Nationality, a State founded on this principle has generally one real practical advantage through its obliteration of small tyrannies and local oppressions. It has further to be observed, that a very serious weakness in Bentham's argument has been disclosed by the experience of half a century, an experience which might be carried much farther back with the help of that historical inquiry which Bentham neglected and perhaps despised. Democratic governments no doubt attempt to legislate and administer in the interests of Democracy, provided only the words are taken to mean the interests which Democracy supposes to be its own. For purposes of actual government, the standard of interest is not any which Bentham would have approved, but

merely popular opinion. Nobody would have acknowledged this more readily than Bentham, if his marvellously
long life could have been prolonged to this day. He was
the ancestor of the advanced Liberals or Radicals who
now carry everything before them. All their favourite
political machinery came from his intellectual workshop.
Household suffrage (which he faintly preferred to universal suffrage), vote by ballot, and the short Parliaments
once in favour, received his energetic advocacy; and he
detested the House of Lords. Yet there is no political
writer whose strongest and most fundamental opinions
are so directly at variance with the Radical ideas of the
moment. One has only to turn over his pages for abundant evidence of this assertion. Over and over again, you
come upon demonstration that all the mechanism of human society depends on the satisfaction of reasonable
expectations, and therefore on the strict maintenance of
proprietary right, and the inviolability of contract. You
find earnest cautions against the hasty acquisition of private property by the State for public advantage, and
vehement protests against the removal of abuses without
full compensation to those interested in them. Amid his
denunciation of these capital vices of the legislator, it is
amusing to read his outbreaks[12] of enthusiasm for the

---

[12] "In England, one of the greatest and best understood improvements is the
inclosure of commons. When we pass over the lands which have undergone
this happy change, we are enchanted as with the appearance of a new colony;
harvests, flocks, and smiling habitations, have now succeeded to the sadness
and sterility of the desert. Happy conquests of peaceful industry! Noble
aggrandisements which inspire no alarms and provoke no enemies!"—Bentham's *Works,* i. 342.

inclosure of commons, now sometimes described as stealing the inheritance of the poor. The very vices of political argument which he was thought to have disposed of for ever have gained a new vitality among the political school he founded. The "Anarchical Sophisms" which he exposed have migrated from France to England, and may be read in the literature of Advanced Liberalism side by side with the Parliamentary Fallacies which he laughed at in the debates of a Tory House of Commons.

The name of Jeremy Bentham, one of the few who have wholly lived for what they held to be the good of the human race, has become even among educated men a byword for what is called his "low view" of human nature. The fact is that, under its most important aspect, he greatly overrated human nature. He overestimated its intelligence. He wrongly supposed that the truths which he saw, clearly cut and distinct, in the dry light of his intellect, could be seen by all other men or by many of them. He did not understand that they were visible only to the Few—to the intellectual aristocracy. His delusion was the greater from his inattention to facts which lay little beyond the sphere of his vision. Knowing little of history, and caring little for it, he neglected one easy method of assuring himself of the extreme falseness of the conceptions of their interest, which a multitude of men may entertain. "The world," said Machiavelli, "is made up of the vulgar." Thus Bentham's fundamental proposition turns against himself. It is that, if you place power in men's hands, they will use it for their interest. Applying the rule to the whole of a political community, we ought to have a perfect system of government; but, taking it in connection with the fact that multitudes include too much ignorance to be capable of understanding their interest, it furnishes the principal argument against Democracy.

The immunity from sinister influences, the freedom from temptation to prefer the smaller interest to the greater, which Bentham claimed for Democracy, should thus have been extended by him to the more absolute forms of Monarchy. If indeed this suggestion had been made to him, he would probably have replied that Monarchy has a tendency to show unjust favours to the military, the official, and the courtly classes, the classes nearest to itself. Monarchy, however, had had a very long history in Bentham's day, and Democracy a very short one; and it is only as the political history of the American Union had developed itself, that we are able to detect in wide popular governments the same infirmities that characterised the kingly governments, of which they are the inverted reproductions. Under the shelter of one government as of the other, all sorts of selfish interests breed and multiply, speculating on its weaknesses and pretending to be its servants, agents, and delegates. Nevertheless, after making all due qualifications, I do not at all deny to Democracies some portion of the advantage which so masculine a thinker as Bentham claimed for them. But, putting this advantage at the highest, it is more than compensated by one great disadvantage. Of all the forms of government, Democracy is by far the most difficult. Little as the governing multitude is conscious of this difficulty, prone as the masses are to aggravate it by their avidity for taking more and more powers into their direct management, it is a fact which experience has placed beyond all dispute. It is the difficulty of democratic government that mainly accounts for its ephemeral duration.

The greatest, most permanent, and most fundamental of all the difficulties of Democracy, lies deep in the constitution of human nature. Democracy is a form of government, and in all governments acts of State are determined by an exertion of will. But in what sense can a multitude exercise volition? The student of politics can put to himself no more pertinent question than this. No doubt the vulgar opinion is, that the multitude makes up its mind as the individual makes up his mind; the Demos determines like the Monarch. A host of popular phrases testify to this belief. The "will of the People," "public opinion," the "sovereign pleasure of the nation," "Vox Populi, Vox Dei," belong to this class, which indeed constitutes a great part of the common stock of the platform and the press. But what do such expressions mean? They must mean that a great number of people, on a great number of questions, can come to an identical conclusion, and found an identical determination upon it. But this is manifestly true only of the simplest questions. A very slight addition of difficulty at once sensibly diminishes the chance of agreement, and, if the difficulty be considerable, an identical opinion can only be reached by trained minds assisting themselves by demonstration more or less rigorous. On the complex questions of politics, which are calculated in themselves to task to the utmost all the powers of the strongest minds, but are in fact vaguely conceived, vaguely stated, dealt with for the most part in the most haphazard manner by the most experienced statesmen, the common determination of a multitude is a chimerical assumption; and indeed, if it were really possible to extract an opinion upon them from a great mass of men, and to shape the administrative and legislative acts of a State upon this opinion as a sovereign command, it is probable that the most ruinous blunders would be committed, and all social progress would be arrested. The truth is, that the modern enthusiasts for Democracy make one fundamental confusion. They mix up the theory, that the Demos is capable of volition, with the fact, that it is capable of adopting the opinions of one man or of a limited number of men, and of founding directions to its instruments upon them.

The fact, that what is called the will of the people really consists in their adopting the opinion of one person or a few persons, admits of a very convincing illustration from experience. Popular Government and Popular Justice were originally the same thing. The ancient democracies devoted much more time and attention to the exercise of civil and criminal jurisdiction than to the administration of their public affairs; and, as a matter of fact, popular justice has lasted longer, has had a more continuous history, and has received much more observation and cultivation, than popular government. Over much of the world it gave way to Royal Justice, which was of at least equal antiquity, but it did not give way as universally or as completely as popular government did to monarchy. We have in England a relic of the ancient Popular Justice in the functions of the Jury. The Jury—technically known as the "country"—is the old adjudicating Democracy, limited, modified, and improved, in accordance with the principles suggested by the experience of centuries, so as to bring it into harmony with modern ideas of judicial efficiency.[13] The change which has had to be made in it is in the highest degree instructive. The Jurors are twelve, instead of a multitude. Their main business is to say "Aye" or "No" on questions which are doubtless important, but which turn on facts arising in the transactions of everyday life. In order that they may reach a conclusion, they are assisted by a system of contrivances and rules of the highest artificiality and elaboration. An expert presides over their investigations—the Judge, the representative of the rival and royal justice—and an entire literature is concerned with the conditions under which evidence on the facts in dispute may be laid before them. There is a rigid exclusion of all testimony which has a tendency to bias them unfairly. They are addressed, as of old, by the litigants or their advocates, but their inquiry concludes with a security unknown to antiquity, the summing-up of the expert President, who is bound by all the rules of his profession to the sternest impartiality. If he errs, or if they flagrantly err, the proceedings may be quashed by a superior Court of experts. Such is Popular Justice, after ages of cultivation. Now it happens that the oldest Greek poet has left us a picture, certainly copied from reality, of what Popular Justice was in its infancy. The primitive Court is sitting; the question is "guilty" or "not guilty." The old men of the community

---

[13] This intricate subject is discussed by Stephen *(History of Criminal Law,* i. 254); Stubbs *(Constitutional History,* i. 685, especially Note 3); Maine *(Early Law and Custom,* p. 160).

give their opinions in turn; the adjudicating Democracy, the commons standing round about, applaud the opinion which strikes them most, and the applause determines the decision. The Popular Justice of the ancient republics was essentially of the same character. The adjudicating Democracy simply followed the opinion which most impressed them in the speech of the advocate or litigant. Nor is it in the least doubtful that, but for the sternly repressive authority of the presiding Judge, the modern English Jury would, in the majority of cases, blindly surrender its verdict to the persuasiveness of one or other of the counsel who have been retained to address it.

A modern governing democracy is the old adjudicating democracy very slightly changed. It cannot indeed be said that no attempt has been made to introduce into the multitudinous government modifications resembling those which have turned the multitudinous tribunal into the Jury, for a variety of expedients for mitigating the difficulty of popular government have been invented and applied in England and the United States. But in our day a movement appears to have very distinctly set in towards unmodified democracy, the government of a great multitude of men striving to take the bulk of their own public affairs into their own hands. Such a government can only decide the questions submitted to it, as the old popular Courts of Justice decided them, by applauding somebody who speaks to it. The ruling multitude will only form an opinion by following the opinion of somebody—it may be of a great party leader—it may be, of a small local politician—it may be, of an organised association—it may be, of an impersonal newspaper. The process of deciding in accordance with plausibilities (in the strict sense of this last word) goes on over an enormous area, growing ever more confused and capricious, and giving results even more ambiguous or inarticulate, as the numbers to be consulted are multiplied.

The most interesting, and on the whole the most successful, experiments in popular government, are those which have frankly recognised the difficulty under which it labours. At the head of these we must place the virtually English discovery of government by Representation, which caused Parliamentary institutions to be preserved in these islands from the destruction which overtook them everywhere else, and to devolve as an inheritance upon the United States. Under this system, when it was in its prime, an electoral body, never in this country extraordinarily large, chose a number of persons to represent it in Parliament, leaving them unfettered by express instructions, but having with them at most a general understanding, that they would strive to give a particular direction to public policy. The effect was to diminish the difficulties of popular government, in exact proportion to the diminution in the number of persons who had to decide public questions. But this famous system is evidently in decay, through the ascendency over it which is being gradually obtained by the vulgar assumption that great masses of men can directly decide all necessary questions for themselves. The agency, by which the representative is sought to be turned into the mere mouthpiece of opinions collected in the locality which sent him to the House of Commons, is, we need hardly say, that which is generally supposed to have been introduced from the United States under the name of the Caucus, but

which had very possibly a domestic exemplar in the ecclesiastical organisation of the Wesleyan Methodists. The
old Italian toxicologists are said to have always arranged
their discoveries in a series of three terms—first the poi-
son, next the antidote, thirdly the drug which neutralised
the antidote. The antidote to the fundamental infirmities
of democracy was Representation, but the drug which
defeats it has now been found in the Caucus. And, by an
unhappy mischance, the rapid conversion of the unfettered representative into the instructed delegate has occurred just at the time when the House of Commons itself
is beginning to feel the inevitable difficulties produced by
its numerousness. Jeremy Bentham used to denounce the
non-attendance of Members of Parliament at all sittings
as a grave abuse; but it now appears that the scanty attendance of members, and the still scantier participation
of most of them in debate, were essential to the conduct
of business by the House of Commons, which was then,
as it is still, the most numerous deliberative Assembly in
the world. The Obstruction spoken of by politicians of
experience with lamentation and surprise is nothing more
than a symptom of the familiar disease of large governing
bodies; it arises from the numbers of the House of Commons, and from the variety of opinions struggling in it
for utterance. The remedies hitherto tried for the cure of
Obstruction will prove, in my judgment, to be merely
palliatives. No multitudinous assembly which seeks
really to govern can possibly be free from it; and it
will probably lead to a constitutional revolution, the
House of Commons abandoning the greatest part of its
legislative authority to a Cabinet of Executive Ministers.

Another experiment, which, like the system of Representation, is founded on the acknowledgment of fundamental difficulties, has been attempted several times in our generation, though not in our country. In one of its forms it has been known as the Plébiscite. A question, or a series of questions, is simplified as much as possible, and the entire enfranchised portion of the community is asked to say "Aye" or "No" to it. The zealots of democracy are beginning to forget, or conveniently to put aside, the enormous majorities by which the French nation, now supposed to be governing itself as a democracy, gave only the other day to a military despot any answer which he desired; but it may be conceded to them that the question put to the voters was not honestly framed, however much it was simplified in form. Whether Louis Napoleon Bonaparte should be President for life with large legislative powers? whether he should be a hereditary Emperor? whether he should be allowed to divest himself of a portion of the authority he had assumed? were not simple, but highly complex questions, incapable of being replied to by a naked "Yes" or "No." But the principle of the Plébiscite has been engrafted on the Swiss Federal Constitution; and in some of the Cantonal Constitutions the "Referendum," as it is called, had existed from an earlier date. Here there is no ground for a charge of dishonesty. A new law is first thoroughly debated, voted upon, and amended, by the Legislature; and the debates are carried by the newspapers to every corner of Swiss territory. But it does not come at once into force. If a certain number of citizens so desire, the entire electoral body is called upon to say "Aye" or "No" to the question whether the law shall become operative. I do not undertake to say that the expedient has failed, but it can only be considered thoroughly successful by those who wish that there should be as little legislation as possible. Contrary to all expectations,[14] to the bitter disappointment of the authors of the Referendum, laws of the highest importance, some of them openly framed for popularity, have been vetoed by the People after they had been adopted by the Federal or Cantonal Legislature. This result is sufficiently intelligible. It is possible, by agitation and exhortation, to produce in the mind of the average citizen a vague impression that he desires a particular change. But, when the agitation has settled down on the dregs, when the excitement has died away, when the subject has been threshed out, when the law is before him with all its detail, he is sure to find in it much that is likely to disturb his habits, his ideas, his prejudices, or his interests; and so, in the long-run, he votes "No" to every proposal. The delusion that Democracy, when it has once had all things put under its feet, is a progressive form of government, lies deep in the convictions of a particular political school; but there can be no delusion grosser. It receives no

---

[14] What these expectations were, may be gathered from the language of M. Numa Droz. M. Droz calls the Referendum "l'essai le plus grandiose qu'une République ait jamais tenté." The effect, however, has been that, since the commencement of the experiment in 1874 there have been vetoed, among other laws passed by the Federal Legislature, an Electoral Law (twice over), a Law on Currency, a Law creating a Department of Education, a Law creating a Department of Justice, a Law providing a salary for a Secretary of Legation at Washington, and a Law permitting the *venue* to be changed to the Federal Court when there is reason to suspect the fairness of a Cantonal tribunal. It is remarkable that, under a Cantonal Referendum, a Law establishing a progressive Income Tax was negatived.

countenance either from experience or from probability. Englishmen in the East come into contact with vast populations of high natural intelligence, to which the very notion of innovation is loathsome; and the very fact that such populations exist should suggest that the true difference between the East and the West lies merely in this, that in Western countries there is a larger minority of exceptional persons who, for good reasons or bad, have a real desire for change. All that has made England famous, and all that has made England wealthy, has been the work of minorities, sometimes very small ones. It seems to me quite certain that, if for four centuries there had been a very widely extended franchise and a very large electoral body in this country, there would have been no reformation of religion, no change of dynasty, no toleration of Dissent, not even an accurate Calendar. The threshing-machine, the power-loom, the spinning-jenny, and possibly the steam-engine, would have been prohibited. Even in our day, vaccination is in the utmost danger, and we may say generally that the gradual establishment of the masses in power is of the blackest omen for all legislation founded on scientific opinion, which requires tension of mind to understand it and self-denial to submit to it.

The truth is, that the inherent difficulties of democratic government are so manifold and enormous that, in large and complex modern societies, it could neither last nor work if it were not aided by certain forces which are not exclusively associated with it, but of which it greatly stimulates the energy. Of these forces, the one to which it owes most is unquestionably Party.

No force acting on mankind has been less carefully examined than Party, and yet none better deserves examination. The difficulty which Englishmen in particular feel about it is very like that which men once experienced when they were told that the air had weight. It enveloped them so evenly and pressed on them so equally, that the assertion seemed incredible. Nevertheless it is not hard to show that Party and Party Government are very extraordinary things. Let us suppose it to be still the fashion to write the apologues so dear to the last century, in which some stranger from the East or West, some Persian full of intelligent curiosity, some Huron still unspoilt by civilisation, or some unprejudiced Bonze from India or China, described the beliefs and usages of European countries, just as they struck him, to his kinsmen at the other end of the world. Let us assume that in one of these trifles, by a Voltaire or a Montesquieu, the traveller gave an account of a cultivated and powerful European Commonwealth, in which the system of government consisted in half the cleverest men in the country taking the utmost pains to prevent the other half from governing. Or let us imagine some modern writer, with the unflinching perspicacity of a Machiavelli, analysing the great Party Hero—leader or agitator—as the famous Italian analysed the personage equally interesting and important in his day, the Tyrant or Prince. Like Machiavelli, he would not stop to praise or condemn on ethical grounds: "he would follow the real truth of things rather than an imaginary view of them."[15] "Many Party Heroes," he would say,

---

[15] *The Prince,* xv (101).

"have been imagined, who were never seen or known to exist in reality." But he would describe them as they really were. Allowing them every sort of private virtue, he would deny that their virtues had any effect on their public conduct, except so far as they helped to make men believe their public conduct virtuous. But this public conduct he would find to be not so much immoral as non-moral. He would infer, from actual observation, that the party Hero was debarred by his position from the full practice of the great virtues of veracity, justice, and moral intrepidity. He could seldom tell the full truth; he could never be fair to persons other than his followers and associates; he could rarely be bold except in the interests of his faction. The picture drawn by him would be one which few living men would deny to be correct, though they might excuse its occurrence in nature on the score of moral necessity. And then, a century or two later, when Democracies were as much forgotten as the Italian Principedoms, our modern Machiavelli would perhaps be infamous and his work a proverb of immorality.

Party has many strong affinities with Religion. Its devotees, like those of a religious creed, are apt to substitute the fiction that they have adopted it upon mature deliberation for the fact that they were born into it or stumbled into it. But they are in the highest degree reluctant to come to an open breach with it; they count it shame to speak of its weak points, except to co-religionists; and, whenever it is in serious difficulty, they return to its assistance or rescue. Their relation to those outside the pale—the relation of Whig to Tory, of Conservative to Liberal—is on the whole exceedingly like that of Jew to Samaritan. But the closest resemblances are between party discipline and military discipline; and indeed, historically speaking, Party is probably nothing more than a survival and a consequence of the primitive combativeness of mankind. It is war without the city transmuted into war within the city, but mitigated in the process. The best historical justification which can be offered for it is that it has often enabled portions of the nation, who would otherwise be armed enemies, to be only factions. Party strife, like strife in arms, develops many high but imperfect and one-sided virtues; it is fruitful of self-denial and self-sacrifice. But wherever it prevails, a great part of ordinary morality is unquestionably suspended; a number of maxims are received, which are not those of religion or ethics; and men do acts which, except as between enemies, and except as between political opponents, would be very generally classed as either immoralities or sins.

Party disputes were originally the occupation of aristocracies, which joined in them because they loved the sport for its own sake; and the rest of the community followed one side or the other as its clients. Now-a-days, Party has become a force acting with vast energy on multitudinous democracies, and a number of artificial contrivances have been invented for facilitating and stimulating its action. Yet, in a democracy, the fragment of political power falling to each man's share is so extremely small, that it would be hardly possible, with all the aid of the Caucus, the Stump, and the Campaign newspaper, to rouse the interests of thousands or millions of men, if Party were not coupled with another political force. This, to speak plainly, is Corruption. A story is current respecting a conversation of the great American, Alexander Hamilton, with a friend who expressed wonder at Hamilton's extreme admiration of so corrupt a system as that covered by the name of the British Constitution. Hamilton is said to have, in reply, expressed his belief that when the corruption came to an end the Constitution would fall to pieces. The corruption referred to was that which had been openly practised by the Whig Ministers of George I and George II through the bestowal of places and the payment of sums of money, but which in the reign of George III had died down to an obscurer set of malpractices, ill-understood, but partially explained by the constant indebtedness of the thrifty King. Hamilton of course meant that, amid the many difficulties of popular government, he doubted whether, in its English form, it could be carried on, unless support were purchased by governments; and this opinion might very plausibly have been held concerning the early governments of the Hanoverian dynasty, so deeply unpopular did the "Revolution Settlement" soon become with large classes of Englishmen. What put an end to this corruption was in reality not an English but a French phenomenon—the Revolution begun in 1789, which, through the violent repulsion with which it inspired the greatest part of the nation, and the half-avowed attraction which it had for the residue, supplied the English parties with principles of action which did not need the co-operation of any corrupt inducement to partisanship. The corruption which we find denounced by Bentham after the close of the great war was not bribery, but vested interest; nor did the old practices ever revive in England in their ancient shape. Votes at elections continued to be bought and sold, but not votes in Parliament.

Whether Hamilton looked forward to an era of purity in his own country, cannot be certainly known. He and his coadjutors undoubtedly were unprepared for the rapid development of Party which soon set in; they evidently thought that their country would be poor; and they probably expected to see all evil influences defeated by the elaborate contrivances of the Federal Constitution. But the United States became rapidly wealthy and rapidly populous; and the universal suffrage of all white men, native-born or immigrant, was soon established by the legislation of the most powerful States. With wealth, population, and widely diffused electoral power, corruption sprang into vigorous life. President Andrew Jackson, proclaiming the principle of "to the victors the spoils," which all parties soon adopted, expelled from office all administrative servants of the United States who did not belong to his faction; and the crowd of persons filling these offices, which are necessarily very numerous in so vast a territory, together with the groups of wealthy men interested in public lands and in the countless industries protected by the Customs tariff, formed an extensive body of contributors from whom great amounts of money were levied by a species of taxation, to be presently expended in wholesale bribery. A reaction against this system carried the present President of the United States into office; but the opinion of almost all the politicians who the other day supported Mr. Blaine bore probably the closest resemblance to Hamilton's opinion about Great

Britain. They were persuaded that the American Party system cannot continue without corruption. It is impossible to lay down M. Scherer's pamphlet[16] without a conviction, that the same opinion is held of France by the public men who direct the public affairs of the French Republic. The account which this writer gives of the expedients by which all French Governments have sought to secure support, since the resignation of Marshal Mac-Mahon, is most deplorable. There is a scale of public corruption, with an excessive and extravagant scheme of public works at one end of it, and at the other the open barter of votes by the electoral committees for the innumerable small places in the gift of the highly centralised French administration. The principle that the spoils belong to the victors has been borrowed from the United States, and receives a thoroughgoing application. Every branch of the public service—even, since M. Scherer wrote, the judicial bench—has been completely purged of functionaries not professing allegiance to the party in power for the time being.

We Englishmen, alone among popularly governed communities, have tried an expedient peculiar to ourselves. We have handed over all patronage to the Civil Service Commissioners, and we have adopted the Corrupt Practices Act. It is a most singular fact, that the only influences having an affinity for the old corruption, which still survive in Great Britain, are such as can be brought to bear on those exalted regions of society, in which stars, garters, ribands, titles, and lord-lieutenancies, still circu-

---

[16] See especially pages 24, 25, 27, 29, 35.

late. What will be the effect on British government of the heroic remedies we have administered to ourselves, has yet to be seen. What will come of borrowing the Caucus from the United States, and refusing to soil our fingers with the oil used in its native country to lubricate the wheels of the machine? Perhaps we are not at liberty to forget that there are two kinds of bribery. It can be carried on by promising or giving to expectant partisans places paid out of the taxes, or it may consist in the directer process of legislating away the property of one class and transferring it to another. It is this last which is likely to be the corruption of these latter days.

Party and Corruption, as influences which have shown themselves capable of bringing masses of men under civil discipline, are probably as old as the very beginning of political life. The savage ferocity of party strife in the Greek States has been described by the great Greek historian in some of his most impressive sentences; and nothing in modern times has approached the proportions of the corruption practised at the elections of the Roman Republic, in spite of all the impediments placed in its way by an earlier form of the Ballot. But in quite recent times a third expedient has been discovered for producing, not indeed agreement, but the semblance of agreement, in a multitude of men. This is generalisation, the trick of rapidly framing, and confidently uttering, general propositions on political subjects. It was once supposed that the power of appreciating general propositions was especially characteristic of the highest minds, which it distinguished from those of a vulgar stamp always immersed in detail and in particulars. Once or twice, indeed, in the course of their intellectual history, mankind have fallen on their knees to worship generalisation; and indeed, without help from it, it is probable that the strongest intellect would not be able to bear the ever-accumulating burden of particular facts. But, in these latter days, a ready belief in generalities has shown itself to be a characteristic, not indeed of wholly uneducated, but of imperfectly educated minds. Meantime, men ambitious of political authority have found out the secret of manufacturing generalities in any number. Nothing can be simpler. All generalisation is the product of abstraction; all abstraction consists in dropping out of sight a certain number of particular facts, and constructing a formula which will embrace the remainder; and the comparative value of general propositions turns entirely on the relative importance of the particular facts selected and of the particular facts rejected. The modern facility of generalisation is obtained by a curious precipitation and carelessness in this selection and rejection, which, when properly carried out, is the only difficult part of the entire process. General formulas, which can be seen on examination to have been arrived at by attending only to particulars few, trivial, or irrelevant, are turned out in as much profusion as if they dropped from an intellectual machine; and debates in the House of Commons may be constantly read, which consisted wholly in the exchange of weak generalities and strong personalities. On a pure Democracy this class of general formulas has a prodigious effect. Crowds of men can be got to assent to general statements, clothed in striking language, but unverified and perhaps incapable of verification; and thus there is formed a sort of sham and pretence of concurrent opinion. There has been a loose acquiescence in a vague proposition, and then the People, whose voice is the voice of God, is assumed to have spoken. Useful as it is to democracies, this levity of assent is one of the most enervating of national habits of mind. It has seriously enfeebled the French intellect. It is most injuriously affecting the mind of England. It threatens little short of ruin to the awakening intellect of India, where political abstractions, founded exclusively upon English facts, and even here requiring qualification, are applied by the educated minority, and by their newspapers, to a society which, through nine-tenths of its structure, belongs to the thirteenth century of the West.

The points which I have attempted to establish are these. Without denying to democratic governments some of the advantages which were claimed for them by the one thinker of the first order who has held Democracy to be in itself a good form of government, I have pointed out that it has the signal disadvantage of being the most difficult of all governments, and that the principal influences by which this difficulty has hitherto been mitigated are injurious either to the morality or to the intellect of the governing multitude. If the government of the Many be really inevitable, one would have thought that the possibility of discovering some other and newer means of enabling it to fulfil the ends for which all governments exist, would have been a question exercising all the highest powers of the strongest minds, particularly in the community which, through the success of its popular institutions, has paved the way for all modern Democracy. Yet hardly anything worth mentioning has been produced on the subject in England or on the Continent. I ought, however, to notice a series of discussions which have long been going on in the little State of Belgium, ending in a remarkable experiment. Alarmed by a reckless agitation for universal suffrage, the best heads in the country have devised an electoral law,[17] which is worthy of the most respectful attention. Under its provisions, an attempt is made to attach the franchise, not only to property, but to proved capacity in all its manifestations, to confer it not simply on the men who contribute a certain amount to the revenue, but on every man who has taken honours at a High School or at College, on everybody who can pass an examination with credit, on every foreman of a workshop or factory. The idea is to confer power not on the Many, but on the strongest among the Many. The experiment, however, is at present confined to Provincial and Communal Elections; and we have yet to see whether an electoral system, which would be attended by peculiar difficulties in England, can be successfully carried out even in Belgium. On the whole, there is only one country in which the question of the safest and most workable form of democratic government has been adequately discussed, and the results of discussion tested by experiment. This is the United States of America. American experience has, I think, shown that, by wise Constitutional provisions thoroughly thought out beforehand, Democracy may be made tolerable. The public powers are carefully defined; the mode in which they are to be exer-

---

[17] *Code Electoral Belge*, p. 289. Provincial and Communal Law of August 24, 1883.

cised is fixed; and the amplest securities are taken that none of the more important Constitutional arrangements shall be altered without every guarantee of caution and every opportunity for deliberation. The expedient is not conclusive, for the Americans, settled in a country of boundless unexhausted wealth, have never been tempted to engage in socialistic legislation; but, as far as it has gone, a large measure of success cannot be denied to it, success which has all but dispelled the old ill-fame of democracies. The short history of the United States has, at the same time, established one momentous negative conclusion. When a democracy governs, it is not safe to leave unsettled any important question concerning the exercise of public powers. I might give many instances of this, but the most conclusive is the War of Secession, which was entirely owing to the omission of the "fathers" to provide beforehand for the solution of certain Constitutional problems, lest they should stir the topic of negro slavery. It would seem that, by a wise Constitution, Democracy may be made nearly as calm as water in a great artificial reservoir; but if there is a weak point anywhere in the structure, the mighty force which it controls will burst through it and spread destruction far and near.

This warning deserves all the attention of Englishmen. They are opening the way to Democracy on all sides. Let them take heed that it be not admitted into a receptacle of loose earth and sand. And, in laying this caution to heart, it would be well for them to consider what sort of a Constitution it is to which they must trust for the limitation of the powers, and the neutralisation of the weaknesses, of the two or three millions of voters who have been admitted to the suffrage, in addition to the multitude enfranchised in 1867. The events of the summer and autumn of 1884 were not reassuring. During all that time, the air was hot and thick with passionate assertions of contradictory opinions. The points on which the controversy turned were points in the construction of the Constitution, and the fact that the ablest men in the country took sides upon them proves them to be unsettled. Nor does there exist any acknowledged authority by which they can be adjudicated upon and decided. It is useless to appeal to the law, for the very charge against the House of Lords was, that the law had been put abusively into operation. It is useless to allege the authority of the electoral body, for the very charge against the House of Commons was, that it did not represent the constituencies. To describe such a dispute as serious, is hardly to do it justice: but, in order to bring into full light the scope and number of the doubtful questions which it proved to exist, I will mention in turn the principal depositaries of public authority in this country—the Crown, the Cabinet, the House of Lords, and the House of Commons —and I will note the various opinions which appear to be held as to the part which each of them should take in legislation by which the structure of the Constitution is altered.

The powers over legislation which the law recognises in the Crown are its power to veto Bills which have passed both the House of Commons and the House of Lords, and its power to dissolve Parliament. The first of these powers has probably been lost through disuse. There is not, at the same time, the smallest reason for supposing that it was abandoned through any inconsistency with popular government. It was not employed, because there was no occasion for employing it. The reigns of the first Hanoverian Sovereigns were periods of activity in foreign policy, and the legislation of the time was utterly insignificant; the King's Government was, moreover, steadily drawing to itself the initiative in legislation, and for more than a century the Kings succeeded on the whole in governing through what Ministers they pleased. As to the right to dissolve Parliament by an independent exercise of the royal will, it cannot be quite confidently asserted to have become obsolete. The question has been much discussed in the Colonies which attempt to follow the British Constitutional procedure, and it seems to be generally allowed that a representative of the Crown cannot be blamed for insisting on a dissolution of the Legislature, though his Ministers are opposed to it. It is probable, however, that in this country the object would be practically attained in a different way. The Crown would appoint Ministers who were willing to take the not very serious risks involved in appealing to the constituencies. The latest precedent in this case is quite modern. William IV, her Majesty's uncle and immediate predecessor, replaced Lord Melbourne by Sir Robert Peel in 1834, and Sir Robert Peel, as he afterwards told the House of Commons, took upon himself the entire responsibility of dissolving Parliament.

The Cabinet, which through a series of Constitutional fictions has succeeded to all the powers of the Crown, has drawn to itself all, and more than all, of the royal power over legislation. It can dissolve Parliament, and, if it were

to advise the Crown to veto a Bill which has been passed
through both Houses, there is no certainty that the proceeding would be seriously objected to. That it can arrest
a measure at any stage of its progress through either
House of Parliament, is conceded on all hands; and indeed
the exercise of this power was exemplified on the largest
scale at the end of the Session of 1884, when a large
number of Bills of the highest importance were abandoned in deference to a Cabinet decision. The Cabinet has
further become the sole source of all important legislation, and therefore, by the necessity of the case, of all
Constitutional legislation; and as a measure amending the
Constitution passes through the House of Commons, the
modification or maintenance of its details depends entirely on the fiat of the Ministers of the day. Although
the Cabinet, as such, is quite unknown to the law, it is
manifestly the English institution which is ever more and
more growing in authority and influence; and already,
besides wielding more than the legislative powers of the
Crown, it has taken to itself nearly all the legislative
powers of Parliament, depriving it in particular of the
whole right of initiation. The long familiarity of Englishmen with this institution, and with the copies of it made
in the European countries which possess Constitutions,
has blinded them to its extreme singularity. There is a
fashion among historians of expressing wonder, not un-
mixed with dislike, at the secret bodies and councils
which they occasionally find invested with authority in
famous States. In ancient history, the Spartan Ephors—in
modern history, the Venetian Council of Ten—are criticised in this spirit. Many of these writers are Englishmen,

and yet they seem quite unconscious that their own country is governed by a secret [18] Council. There can be very little doubt that the secrecy of the Cabinet is its strength. A great part of the weakness of Democracy springs from publicity of discussion; and nobody who has had any share in public business can have failed to observe, that the chances of agreement among even a small number of persons increase in nearly exact proportion to the chances of privacy. If the growth in power of the Cabinet is checked, it will probably be from causes of very recent origin. It is essentially a committee of the men who lead the party which has a majority in the House of Commons. But there are signs that its authority over its party is passing to other committees, selected less for eminence in debate and administration than for the adroit management of local political business.

The House of Lords, as a matter of strict law, has the right to reject or amend any measure which is submitted to it; nor has this legal right in either of its forms been disused or abandoned, save as regards money-bills. But it has lately become evident that, when the right is exerted over measures amending the Constitution, strong differences of opinion exist as to the mode and conditions of its exercise; and, as is not uncommon in this country,

---

[18] No secret has been better kept than that of English Cabinet procedure. Apart from Cabinet Ministers, past and present, there are probably not a dozen men in the country who know accurately how Cabinets conduct their deliberations, and how they arrive at a conclusion. Some information may, however, be obtained from the published Diaries of the second Lord Ellenborough, from some printed, but unpublished, Memoirs left by Lord Broughton (Sir J. Cam Hobhouse), and in some degree from Lord Malmesbury's recent *Memoirs of an ex-Minister*.

it is very difficult to gather from the violent language of the disputants, whether they contend that the law should be altered, or that the exertion of power with which they are quarrelling is forbidden by usage, precedent, conventional understanding, or mere expediency. The varieties of doctrine are many and wide apart. On the one hand, one extreme party compares the rejection of a Bill by the House of Lords to the veto of a Bill by the Crown, and insists that the first power should be abandoned as completely as the last is believed to have been. Conversely, the most influential[19] members of the House of Lords allow that it would act improperly in rejecting a constitutional measure, of which the electoral body has signified its approval by the result of a general election. Between these positions there appear to be several intermediate opinions, most of them, however, stated in language of the utmost uncertainty and vagueness. Some persons appear to think that the House of Lords ought not to reject or postpone a constitutional measure which affects the powers of the House of Commons, or its relation to the constituencies, or the constituencies themselves. Others seem to consider that the power of rejection might be exercised on such a measure, if the majority by which it has passed the House of Commons is small, but not if it exceeds a certain number. Lastly, little can be extracted from the language of a certain number of controversialists, violent as it is, except an opinion that the House of

---

[19] Lord Salisbury strongly urged this principle upon the House of Lords when the Bill for disestablishing and disendowing the Established Church of Ireland was before it. This speech probably secured the passing of the Bill.

Lords ought not to do wrong, and that it did wrong on one particular occasion.

The power of the House of Commons over legislation, including constitutional legislation, might seem at first sight to be complete and unqualified. Nevertheless, as I have pointed out, it some time ago surrendered the initiative in legislation, and it is now more and more surrendering the conduct of it, to the so-called Ministers of the Crown. It may further be observed from the language of those who, on the whole, contend for the widest extension of its powers, that a new theory has made its appearance, which raises a number of embarrassing questions as to the authority of the House of Commons in constitutional legislation. This is the theory of the Mandate. It seems to be conceded that the electoral body must supply the House of Commons with a Mandate to alter the Constitution. It has been asserted that a Mandate to introduce Household Suffrage into the counties was given to the House of Commons elected in 1880, but not a Mandate to confer the suffrage on Women. What is a Mandate? As used here, the word has not the meaning which belongs to it in English, French, or Latin. I conjecture that it is a fragment of a French phrase, *mandat impératif,* which means an express direction from a constituency which its representative is not permitted to disobey, and I imagine the mutilation to imply that the direction may be given in some loose and general manner. But in what manner? Is it meant that, if a candidate in an election address declares that he is in favour of household suffrage or woman suffrage, and is afterwards elected, he has a mandate to vote for it, but not otherwise? And, if so, how many election addresses, containing such references, and how many returns, constitute a Mandate to the entire House of Commons? Again, assuming the Mandate to have been obtained, how long is it in force? The House of Commons may sit for seven years under the Septennial Act; but the strict law has hardly ever prevailed, and in the great majority of cases the House of Commons has not lasted for nearly the whole period. May it give effect to its Mandate in its fourth, or fifth, or sixth Session, or must an alteration of the Constitution be the earliest measure to which a Parliament commissioned to deal with it must address itself?

These unsettled questions formed the staple of the controversy which raged among us for months, but the prominence which they obtained is not in the very least arbitrary or accidental. The question of the amount and nature of the notice which the electoral body shall receive of an intended change in the Constitution; the question whether anything like a "Mandate" shall be given by that body to the Legislature; the question whether existing constituencies shall have full jurisdiction over proposed constitutional innovation; the question of the majority which shall be necessary for the decision of the Legislature on a constitutional measure; all these questions belong to the very essence of constitutional doctrine. There is no one of them which is peculiar to this country; what is peculiar to this country is the extreme vagueness with which all of them are conceived and stated. The Americans of the United States, feeling on all sides the strongest pressure of Democracy, but equipped with a remarkable wealth of constitutional knowledge inherited from their forefathers, have had to take up and solve every one of them. I will endeavour to show what have been their methods of solution. I will not at present go for an example to the Constitution of the United States, abounding as it does in the manifold restrictions thought necessary by its framers for the purpose of securing in a probably democratic society the self-command without which it could not become or remain a nation. It will be sufficient for my object to quote the provisions respecting the procedure to be followed on constitutional amendments, contained in the Constitutions of individual States, which, I need not say, can only legislate within the limits permitted to them by the Federal Constitution. One of the subjects, however, on which the powers of the several States were till lately exclusive and are still most extensive, is the Franchise; and this gives a peculiar value and interest to the provisions which I will proceed to extract from the Constitution of the great State of New York.

Article 13 of the Constitution of New York, which is still in force, runs as follows:

> Any amendment or amendments to this Constitution may be proposed to the Senate and Assembly; and if the same be agreed to by a majority of the members elected to each of the two Houses, such amendment or amendments shall be entered on their journals with the "Yeas" and "Nays" taken thereon, and referred to the Legislature to be chosen at the next general election, and shall be published for three months previous to the time of making such choice; and if, in the Legislature so next chosen as aforesaid, such proposed amendment or amendments shall be agreed to by a majority of all the members elected to each House, then it shall be the duty of the Legislature to submit such proposed amendment or amendments to the people in such

manner and at such time as the Legislature shall prescribe; and if the people shall approve and ratify such amendment or amendments by a majority of the electors qualified to vote for members of the Legislature voting thereon, such amendment or amendments shall become part of the Constitution.

Section 2 of the Article provides an alternative mode of amendment.

At the general election to be held (in each twentieth year), and also at such time as the Legislature may by law provide, the question "Shall there be a Convention to revise the Constitution and amend the same?" shall be decided by the electors qualified to vote for members of the Legislature, and in case a majority of the electors so qualified voting at such election shall decide in favour of a Convention for such purpose, the Legislature at the next Session shall provide by law for the election of delegates to such Convention.

These provisions of the Constitution of New York, regulating the procedure to be followed in constitutional amendments, and therefore in measures extending or altering the electoral franchise, are substantially repeated in the Constitutions of nearly all the American States. Where there are variations, they are generally in the direction of greater stringency. The Constitution of Ohio, for example, requires that there shall be at the least a three-fifths majority in each branch of the Legislature proposing an amendment, and a two-thirds majority is necessary if it is sought to summon a Convention. When an amendment is proposed in Massachusetts, a two-thirds majority is demanded in the Lower House; and the same majority must be obtained in both Houses before the Constitution of Louisiana can be amended. The Constitution of New Jersey gives greater precision to the provision of the New York Constitution for the ultimate ratification of the proposed amendment by the constituencies, by inserting, after the words "the people shall ratify and approve," the words "at a special election to be held for that purpose only." The same Constitution declares that "no amendment shall be submitted to the people more than once in five years"; and, like the Constitutions of several other States, it gives no power to summon a revising Convention.

No doubt therefore is possible as to the mode in which these American State Constitutions settle the formidable questions which the discussion of 1884 has shown to be unsettled in this country. First of all, it is to be noted that the electoral body recognised by all the Constitutions, without exception, as having an exclusive jurisdiction over amendments of the Constitution, is the existing electoral body, and not any electoral body of the future. Next, the most ample notice is given to it that an amendment of the Constitution will be brought before the next Legislature which it is called upon to choose; both branches of the outgoing Legislature must record a resolution with the numbers of the division upon it, and this resolution must be published three months before a general election. It is quite clear, therefore, that the representatives chosen at this election will have what may be called a "Mandate." The amendment must then be agreed to by an absolute majority of the members of both Houses of the new Legislature; or, as is required in some States, by a two-thirds or three-fifths majority in both Houses, or one of them. But there is a final security in addition. The

Mandate must be ratified. The amendment must be submitted to the people in any way which the Legislature
may provide; and, as is shown by the Constitution of
New Jersey, the ratification is usually placed in the hands
of a special legislature specially elected for the purpose
of giving or refusing it.

Such are the securities against surprise or haste in conducting the most important part of legislation, which
American political sagacity has devised. They may very
well suggest to the English politician some serious reflections. What was most remarkable in the discussion of
twelve months since was, far less the violent and inflam-
matory language in which it was carried on, than the
extreme vagueness of the considerations upon which it
has turned. The House of Lords, for instance, was threatened with extinction or mutilation for a certain offence.
Yet when the offence is examined, it appears to have
consisted in the violation of some rule or understanding,
never expressed in writing, at variance with the strict law,
and not perhaps construed in precisely the same way by
any two thinking men in the country. Political history
shows that men have at all times quarrelled more fiercely
about phrases and formulas, than even about material
interests; and it would seem that the discussion of British
Constitutional legislation is distinguished from the discussion of all other legislation by having no fixed points
to turn upon, and therefore by its irrational violence. Is
it therefore idle to hope that at some calmer moment—
now that the creation of two or three million more voters
has been accomplished—we may borrow a few of the
American securities against surprise and irreflection in

constitutional legislation, and express them with something like the American precision? Is it always to be possible in this country that a great amendment of the Constitution should, first of all, be attempted to be carried by
tumultuary meetings of the population, enfranchised and
unenfranchised—next, that it should be conducted
through Parliament by a process which practically excluded Parliament from all share in shaping its provisions
—and, lastly, that it should hardly become law before it
was hurriedly altered for the purpose of giving votes to
a particular class of paupers? Some have supposed that
the only remedy would be one which involved the conversion of the unwritten Constitution of Great Britain
into a written Constitution. But a great part of our Constitution is already written. Many of the powers of the
Crown—many of the powers of the House of Lords, including the whole of its judicial powers—much of the
constitution of the House of Commons and its entire
relation to the electoral body—have long since been defined by Act of Parliament. There does not seem to be any
insuperable objection, first of all, to making a distinction
between ordinary legislation and legislation which in any
other country would be called Constitutional; and next,
to requiring for the last a special legislative procedure,
intended to secure caution and deliberation, and as near
an approach to impartiality as a system of party government will admit of. The alternative is to leave unsettled
all the questions which the controversy of 1884 brought
to light, and to give free play to a number of tendencies
already actively at work. It is quite plain whither they are
conducting us. We are drifting towards a type of govern-

ment associated with terrible events—a single Assembly, armed with full powers over the Constitution, which it may exercise at pleasure. It will be a theoretically all-powerful Convention, governed by a practically all-powerful secret Committee of Public Safety, but kept from complete submission to its authority by Obstruction, for which its rulers are always seeking to find a remedy in some kind of moral guillotine.

ESSAY III

THE AGE OF PROGRESS

There is no doubt that some of the most inventive, most polite, and best instructed portions of the human race are at present going through a stage of thought which, if it stood by itself, would suggest that there is nothing of which human nature is so tolerant, or so deeply enamoured, as the transformation of laws and institutions. A series of political and social changes, which a century ago no man would have thought capable of being effected save by the sharp convulsion of Revolution, is now contemplated by the bulk of many civilised communities as sure to be carried out, a certain number of persons regarding the prospect with exuberant hope, a somewhat larger number with equanimity, many more with indifference or resignation. At the end of the last century, a Revolution in France shook the whole civilised world; and the consequence of the terrible events and bitter disappointments which it brought with it was to arrest all improvement in Great Britain for thirty years, merely because it was innovation. But in 1830 a second explosion occurred in France, followed by the reconstruction of the British electorate in 1832, and with the British Reformed Parliament began that period of continuous legislation through which, not this country alone, but all Western Europe appears to be passing. It is not often recognised how excessively rare in the world was sustained legislative activity till rather more than fifty years ago, and thus sufficient attention has not been given to some characteristics of this particular mode of exercising sovereign power, which we call Legislation. It has obviously many advantages over Revolution as an instrument of change; while it has quite as trenchant an edge, it is milder, juster, more equable, and sometimes better considered. But in one respect, as at present understood, it may prove to be more dangerous than revolution. Political insanity takes strange forms, and there may be some persons in some countries who look forward to "The Revolution" as implying a series of revolutions. But, on the whole, a Revolution is regarded as doing all its work at once. Legislation, however, is contemplated as neverending. One stage of it is doubtless more or less distinctly conceived. It will not be arrested till the legislative power itself, and all kinds of authority at any time exercised by States, have been vested in the People, the Many, the great majority of the human beings making up each community. The prospect beyond that is dim, and perhaps will prove to be as fertile in disappointment as is always the morrow of a Revolution. But doubtless the popular expectation is that, after the establishment of a Democracy, there will be as much reforming legislation as ever.

This zeal for political movement, gradually identifying itself with a taste for Democracy, has not as yet fully had its way in all societies of Western Europe. But it has greatly affected the institutions of some of them; even when it is checked or arrested, it is shared by considerable minorities of their population; and when (as in Russia) these minorities are very small, the excessive concentration of the passion for change has a manifest tendency to make it dangerously explosive. The analogies to this state of feeling in the Past must be sought rather in the history of Religion than in the history of Politics. There is some resemblance between the period of political reform in the nineteenth century and the period of religious reformation in the sixteenth. Now, as then, the multitude of followers must be distinguished from the smaller group of leaders. Now, as then, there are a certain number of zealots who desire that truth shall prevail. Some of them conceive the movement which they stimulate as an escape from what is distinctly bad; others as an advance from what is barely tolerable to what is greatly better; and a few as an ascent to an ideal state, sometimes conceived by them as a state of Nature, and sometimes as a condition of millennial blessedness. But, behind these, now as then, there is a crowd which has imbibed a delight in change for its own sake, who would reform the Suffrage, or the House of Lords, or the Land Laws, or the Union with Ireland, in precisely the same spirit in which the mob behind the reformers of religion broke the nose of a saint in stone, or made a bonfire of copes and surplices, or shouted for the government of the Church by presbyteries. The passion for religious reform is, however, far more intelligible than the passion for political change, as we now see it in operation. In an intensely believing society, the obligation to think aright was enforced by tremendous penalties; and the sense of this obligation was the propelling force of the Reformation, as at an earlier date it had been the propelling force of the rise and spread of Christianity. But what propelling force is there behind the present political movement, of such inherent energy that it not only animates the minority, who undoubtedly believe in their theories of democracy, or reform, or regeneration, but even makes itself felt by the multitude which reasons blindly or does not reason at all? "If you have wrong ideas about Justification, you shall perish everlastingly," is a very intelligible proposition; but it is not exactly a proposition of the same order as that into which most English democratic philosophy translates itself: "If you vote straight with the Blues, your great-grandchild will be on a level with the average citizen of the United States." The truth seems to be, that a great number of persons are satisfied to think that democracy is inevitable and the democratic movement irresistible; which means that the phenomenon exists, that they see no way of arresting it, and that they feel no inclination to throw themselves in its way. There are others who appear to think that when a man submits to the inevitable it is "greatly to his credit"; as it was to Mr. Gilbert's nautical hero to remain an Englishman because he was born an Englishman. So they baptise the movement with various complimentary names, of which the commonest is Progress, a word of which I have never seen any definition, and which seems to have all sorts of meanings, many of them extraordinary; for some politicians in our day appear to employ it for mere aimless movement, while others actually use it for movement backwards, towards a state of primitive nature.

It is an inquiry of considerable interest, whether the passion for change which has possession of a certain number of persons in this age, and the acquiescence in it which characterises a much larger number, are due to any exceptional causes affecting the sphere of politics, or whether they are universal and permanent phenomena of human nature. There are some striking facts which appear to point to the first conclusion as the more correct. The most remarkable is the relatively small portion of the human race which will so much as tolerate a proposal or attempt to change its usages, laws, and institutions. Vast populations, some of them with a civilisation considerable but peculiar, detest that which in the language of the West would be called reform. The entire Mahommedan world detests it. The multitudes of coloured men who swarm in the great Continent of Africa detest it, and it is detested by that large part of mankind which we are accustomed to leave on one side as barbarous or savage. The millions upon millions of men who fill the Chinese Empire loathe it and (what is more) despise it. There are few things more remarkable and, in their way, more instructive, than the stubborn incredulity and disdain which a man belonging to the cultivated part of Chinese society opposes to the vaunts of Western civilisation which he frequently hears; and his confidence in his own ideas is alike proof against his experience of Western military superiority and against that spectacle of the scientific inventions and discoveries of the West which overcame the exclusiveness of the undoubtedly feebler Japanese. There is in India a minority, educated at the feet of English politicians and in books saturated with English political ideas, which has learned to repeat their language; but it is doubtful whether even these, if they had a voice in the matter, would allow a finger to be laid on the very subjects with which European legislation is beginning to concern itself, social and religious usage. There is not, however, the shadow of a doubt that the enormous mass of the Indian population hates and dreads change, as is natural in the parts of a body-social solidified by caste. The chief difficulty of Indian government is even less the difficulty of reconciling this strong and abiding sentiment with the fainter feeling of the Anglicised minority, than the practical impossibility of getting it understood by the English people. It is quite evident that the greatest fact in Anglo-Indian history, the Mutiny of the mercenary Sepoy Army, is as much a mystery to the average man of the West as are certain colours to the colour-blind; and even historians are compelled to supply wholly or partially fictitious explanations of the events of 1857 to a public which cannot be brought to believe that a vast popular uprising was produced by a prejudice about a greased cartridge. The intense conservatism of much the largest part of mankind is, however, attested by quite as much evidence as is the pride of certain nations in railways, electric telegraphs, or democratic governments.

In spite of overwhelming evidence [I wrote in 1861], it is most difficult for a citizen of Western Europe to bring thoroughly

home to himself the truth that the civilisation which surrounds
him is a rare exception in the history of the world. The tone of
thought common among us, all our hopes, fears, and speculations, would be materially affected, if we had vividly before us
the relation of the progressive races to the totality of human life.
It is indisputable that much the greatest part of mankind has
never shown a particle of desire that its civil institutions should
be improved, since the moment when external completeness was
first given to them by their embodiment in some permanent
record. One set of usages has occasionally been violently overthrown and superseded by another; here and there a primitive
code, pretending to a supernatural origin, has been greatly extended and distorted into the most surprising forms; but, except
in a small section of the world, there has been nothing like the
gradual amelioration of a legal system. There has been material
civilisation, but instead of the civilisation expanding the law, the
law has limited the civilisation.[1]

To the fact that the enthusiasm for change is comparatively rare must be added the fact that it is extremely
modern. It is known but to a small part of mankind, and
to that part but for a short period during a history of
incalculable length. It is not older than the free employment of legislation by more popular governments. There
are few historical errors more serious than the assumption
that popular governments have always been legislating
governments. Some of them, no doubt, legislated on a
scale which would now be considered extremely moderate; but, on the whole, their vigour has shown itself in
struggles to restore or maintain some ancient constitution,
sometimes lying far back in a partly real and partly imaginary Past, sometimes referred to a wholly unhistorical

---

[1] *Ancient Law,* chap. ii., pp. 22, 23. These opinions were adopted by Mr. Grote.
See his *Plato,* vol. ii., chap. v., p. 253 (note).

state of nature, sometimes associated with the great name of an original legislator. We, Englishmen, have had for several centuries a government in which there was a strong popular element, and for two centuries we have had a nearly unqualified popular government.[2] Yet what our forefathers contended for was not a typical constitution in the Future, but a typical constitution in the Past. Our periods of what would now be called legislative reforming activity have been connected with moments, not of violent political but of violent religious emotion—with the outbreak of feeling at the Reformation, with the dominion of Cromwell and the Independents (the true precursors of the modern Irreconcileables), and with the revival of dread and dislike of the Roman Catholic Church during the reign of James II. During the period at which English popular government was attracting to itself the admiration of the educated classes throughout the civilised world, the Parliament of our Hanoverian Kings was busy with controlling executive action, with the discussion of foreign policy, with vehement debates on foreign wars; but it hardly legislated at all. The truth is that the enthusiasm for legislative change took its rise, not in a popularly governed but in an autocratically governed country, not in England but in France. The English political institutions, so envied and panegyrised on the Continent, could not be copied without sweeping legislative innovations, but the grounds and principles on which these innovations were demanded were, as we shall see, wholly unlike anything known to any class of English

---

[2] See above, p. 33.

politicians. Nevertheless, in their final effects, these French ideas have deeply leavened English political thought, mixing with another stream of opinion which is of recent but still of English origin.

An absolute intolerance even of that description of change which in modern language we call political thus characterises much the largest part of the human race, and has characterised the whole of it during the largest part of its history. Are there then any reasons for thinking that the love for change which in our day is commonly supposed to be overpowering, and the capacity for it which is vulgarly assumed to be infinite, are, after all, limited to a very narrow sphere of human action, that which we call politics, and perhaps not even to the whole of this sphere? Let us look at those parts of human nature which have no points of contact with politics, because the authority of the sovereign state is not brought to bear upon them at all, or at most remotely and indirectly. Let us attend for a moment to human Habits, those modes of conduct and behaviour which we follow either quite unconsciously or with no better reason to assign for them than that we have always followed them. Do we readily change our habits? Man is a creature of habit, says an adage which doubtless sums up a vast experience. It is true that the tenacity with which men adhere to habit is not precisely the same in all parts of the globe. It is strictest in the East. It is relaxed in the West, and of all races the English and their descendants, the Americans, are least reluctant to submit to a considerable change of habit for what seems to them an adequate end. Yet the exception is one of the sort which proves the rule. The Englishman, who transports himself to Australia or to India, surrounds himself, under the greatest difficulties, with as close an imitation of English life as he can contrive, and submits all the while to a distasteful exile in the hope of some day returning to the life which he lived in his youth or childhood, though under somewhat more favourable conditions. The truth is that men do alter their habits, but within narrow limits, and almost always with more or less of reluctance and pain. And it is fortunate for them that they are so constituted, for most of their habits have been learned by the race to which they belong through long experience, and probably after much suffering. A man cannot safely eat or drink, or go downstairs, or cross a street, unless he be guided and protected by habits which are the long result of time. One set in particular of these habits, and perhaps the most surprising, that which enables us to deal safely with the destructive element of fire, was probably not acquired by mankind without infinite pain and injury. And all this, for all we know, may be true of the public usages which men follow in common with their fellows.

Let us turn from Habits to Manners, that is, to those customs of behaviour which we not only practise ourselves, but expect other men to follow. Do these suggest that men are naturally tolerant of departure from a usage or an accustomed line of conduct? Rarely; as the subject is examined, it is a very curious one. What is the exact source of the revulsion of feeling which is indubitably caused by a solecism in manners or speech, and of the harshness of the judgment passed on it? Why should the unusual employment of a fork or a finger-glass, or the mispronunciation of a vowel or an aspirate, have the effect of instantly quenching an appreciable amount of human sympathy? Some things about the sentiment are certain. It is not modern, but very ancient, and probably as old as human nature. The incalculably ancient distinctions between one race and another, between Greek and Barbarian, with all the mutual detestation they carried with them, appear to have been founded originally on nothing more than dislike of differences in speech. Again, the sentiment is not confined to the idle and possibly superfine regions of society. It goes down to the humblest social spheres, where, though the code of manners is different, it is even more rigidly enforced. Whatever else these facts may suggest, they assuredly do not suggest the changeableness of human nature.

There are, however, other facts, even more remarkable and instructive, which point to the same conclusion. One half of the human race—at this moment and in our part of the world, the majority of it—have hitherto been kept aloof from politics; nor, till quite recently, was there any evidence that any portion of this body of human beings cared more to embark in politics than to engage in war. There is therefore in all human societies a great and influential class, everywhere possessed of intellectual power, and here of intellectual cultivation, which is essentially non-political. Are, then, Women characterised by a passion for change? Surely there is no fact witnessed to by a greater amount of experience than that, in all communities, they are the strictest conservators of usage and the sternest censors of departure from accepted rules of morals, manners, and fashions. *Souvent femme varie,* says indeed

the French song attributed to Francis I; but subtler observers of female nature than a French king of extraordinary dissoluteness have come to a very different conclusion, and, even in the relations of the sexes, have gone
near to claiming constancy as a special and distinctive
female virtue. This seems to have been an article of faith
with Thackeray and Trollope, but the art which Thackeray and Trollope followed is itself furnishing striking
illustrations of the conservatism of Women. During the
last fifteen years, it has fallen very largely into their
hands. What, then, is the view of life and society which
is taken on the whole by this literature of Fiction, produced in enormous and ever-growing abundance, and
read by multitudes? I may at least say that, if no other
part of the writings of this generation survived, the very
last impression which this branch of literature would produce would be that we had lived in an age of feverish
Progress. For in the world of novels, it is the ancient and
time-hallowed that seems, as a rule, to call forth admiration or enthusiasm; the conventional distinctions of society have a much higher importance given to them than
belongs to them in real life; wealth is on the whole regarded as ridiculous, unless associated with birth; and
zeal for reform is in much danger of being identified with
injustice, absurdity, or crime. These books, ever more
written by Women, and read by increasing multitudes of
Women, leave no doubt as to the fundamental character
of female taste and opinion. It must be admitted, on the
other hand, that one special set of customs, which we
know collectively as Fashion, has been left to the peculiar
guardianship of Women, and there is no doubt a common

impression that Fashion is always changing. But is it true
that fashions vary very widely and very rapidly? Doubtless they do change. In some of the great cities of Europe
something like real genius is called into activity, and
countless experiments are tired, in order that something
may be devised which is new, and yet shall not shock the
strong attachment to the old. Much of this ingenuity fails,
some part of it sometimes succeeds; yet the change is very
seldom great, and it is just as often a reversion to the old
as an adoption of something new. "We speak," I said in
a former work, "of the caprices of Fashion; yet, on examining them historically, we find them extraordinarily limited, so much so that we are sometimes tempted to regard
Fashion as passing through cycles of form ever repeating
themselves."[3] The eccentricities of female dress mentioned in the Old Testament may still be recognised; the
Greek lady represented by the so-called Tanagra figures[4]
is surprisingly like a lady of our time; and, on looking
through a volume of mediaeval costumes, we see portions
of dress which, slightly disguised, have been over and
over again revived by the dressmaking inventiveness of
Paris. Here, again, we may observe that it is extremely
fortunate for a large part of the human race that female
fashions do not alter extensively and rapidly. For sudden
and frequent changes in them—changes which would
more or less affect half of mankind in the wealthiest
regions of the world—would entail industrial revolutions

---

[3] I quote the whole of the passage in which this sentence occurs in Note A
appended to this chapter.
[4] The chief differences are that the Greek lady is without stays, and occasionally wears a parasol as a fixed part of her headdress.

of the most formidable kind. One may ask oneself what is the most terrible calamity which can be conceived as befalling great populations. The answer might perhaps be—a sanguinary war, a desolating famine, a deadly epidemic disease. Yet none of these disasters would cause as much and as prolonged human suffering as a revolution in fashion under which women should dress, as men practically do, in one material of one colour. There are many flourishing and opulent cities in Europe and America which would be condemned by it to bankruptcy or starvation, and it would be worse than a famine or a pestilence in China, India, and Japan.

This view of the very slight changeableness of human nature when left to itself, is much strengthened by the recent inquiries which have extended the history of the human race in new directions. The investigations inconveniently called prehistoric are really aimed at enlarging the domain of history, by collecting materials for it beyond the point at which it began to be embodied in writing. They proceed by the examination of the modes of life and social usages of men in a savage, barbarous, or semi-civilised condition, and they start from the assumption that the civilised races were once in that state, or in some such state. Unquestionably, these studies are not in a wholly satisfactory stage. As often happens where the labourers are comparatively few and the evidence as yet scanty, they abound in rash conclusions and peremptory assertions. But they have undoubtedly increased our knowledge of social states which are no longer ours, and of civilisations which are unlike ours. And on the whole, they suggest that the differences which, after ages of change, separate the civilised man from the savage or barbarian, are not so great as the vulgar opinion would have them. Man has changed much in Western Europe, but it is singular how much of the savage there still is in him, independently of the identity of the physical constitution which has always belonged to him. There are a number of occupations which civilised men follow with the utmost eagerness, and a number of tastes in which they indulge with the keenest pleasure, without being able to account for them intellectually, or to reconcile them with accepted morality. These pursuits and tastes are, as a rule, common to the civilised man and the savage. Like the savage, the Englishman, Frenchman, or American makes war; like the savage, he hunts; like the savage, he dances; like the savage, he indulges in endless deliberation; like the savage, he sets an extravagant value on rhetoric; like the savage, he is a man of party, with a newspaper for a totem, instead of a mark on his forehead or arm; and like a savage, he is apt to make of his totem his God. He submits to having these tastes and pursuits denounced in books, speeches, or sermons; but he probably derives acuter pleasure from them than from anything else he does.

If, then, there is any reason for supposing that human nature, taken as a whole, is not wedded to change, and that, in most of its parts, it changes only by slow steps, or within narrow limits—if the maxim of Seneca be true of it, *non fit statim ex diverso in diversum transitus*—it is worth our while to investigate the probable causes of the exceptional enthusiasm for change in politics which seems to grow up from time to time, giving to many minds the sense of having in their presence an inflexible, inexorable, predetermined process. I may first observe that, in the popular mind, there is a manifest association of political innovation with scientific advance. It is not uncommon to hear a politician supporting an argument for a radical reform by asserting that this is an Age of Progress, and appealing for proof of the assertion to the railway, the gigantic steamship, the electric light, or the electric telegraph. Now it is quite true that, if Progress be understood with its only intelligible meaning, that is, as the continued production of new ideas, scientific invention and scientific discovery are the great and perennial sources of these ideas. Every fresh conquest of Nature by man, giving him the command of her forces, and every new and successful interpretation of her secrets, generates a number of new ideas, which finally displace the old ones, and occupy their room. But, in the Western world, the mere formation of new ideas does not often or necessarily create a taste for innovating legislation. In the East, no doubt, it is otherwise. Where a community associates the bulk of its social usages with a religious sanction, and again associates its religion with an old and false interpretation of Nature, the most elementary knowledge of geography or physics may overthrow a mass of fixed ideas concerning the constitution of society. An Indian youth learns that a Brahman is semi-divine, and that it is a deadly sin to taste the flesh of a cow, but he also learns that Ceylon, which is close to India, is an island peopled with demons; and the easy exposure of such delusions may change his entire view of human life, and indeed is the probable explanation of the great gulf which in India divides the educated class from the uneducated. A similar revolution of ideas is very rare in the West, and indeed experience shows that innovating legislation is connected not so much with Science as with the scientific air which certain subjects, not capable of exact scientific treatment, from time to time assume. To this class of subjects belonged Bentham's scheme of Law-Reform, and, above all, Political Economy as treated by Ricardo. Both have been extremely fertile sources of legislation during the last fifty years. But both have now fallen almost entirely out of fashion; and their present disfavour may serve as a warning against too hastily assuming that the existing friendly alliance between advanced politicians and advancing science will always continue. When invention has been successfully applied to the arts of life, the disturbance of habits and displacement of industries, which the application occasions, has always been at first profoundly unpopular. Men have submitted to street-lighting and railway-travelling, which they once clamoured against; but Englishmen never submitted to the Poor Law—the first great effort of economical legislation—and it has got to be seen whether they will submit to Free Trade. The prejudices of the multitude against scientific inventions are dismissed by the historian[5] with a sarcasm; but, when the multitude is all-powerful, this prejudice may afford material for history.

The principal cause of an apparent enthusiasm for in-

---

[5] Macaulay, *History*, I., c. iii., p. 283. "There were fools in that age (1685) who opposed the introduction of what was called the new light, as strenuously as fools in our age have opposed the introduction of vaccination and railroads."

novating legislation is not as often assigned as it should
be. Legislation is one of the activities of popular government; and the keenest interest in these activities is felt
by all the popularly governed communities. It is one great
advantage of popular government over government of the
older type, that it is so intensely interesting. For twenty
years, we had close to our shores a striking example of
this point of inferiority in absolute monarchies during the
continuance of the Second Bonapartist Empire in France.
It never overcame the disadvantage it suffered through
the dullness of its home politics. The scandal, the personalities, the gossip, and the trifling which occupied its
newspapers proved no substitute for the political discussions which had filled them while the Republic and the
Constitutional Monarchy lasted. The men who ruled it
were acutely conscious of the danger involved in this
decline of excitement and amusement suitable to cultivated and masculine minds; and their efforts to meet it
led directly to their overthrow, by tempting them to provide the French public with distractions of a higher order,
through adventurous diplomacy and war. There are,
again, good observers who trace the political insecurity
of Russia, the aggressiveness of her government abroad,
and the wild attempts on it at home, to the general dullness of Russian life during peace. Englishmen would find
it almost impossible to conceive what would compensate
them for the withdrawal of the enthralling drama which
is enacted before them every morning and evening. A
ceaseless flow of public discussion, a throng of public
events, a crowd of public men, make up the spectacle.
Nevertheless, in our country at all events, over-indul-

gence in what has no doubt become a passion with elevated minds is growing to be dangerous. For the plot of the performance which attracts such multitudes turns, now-a-days, almost always on the fortunes of some legislative measure. The English Parliament, as has been said, legislated very little until fifty years since, when it fell under the influence of Bentham and his disciples. Ever since the first Reform Act, however, the volume of legislation has been increasing, and this has been very much owing to the unlooked-for-operation of a venerable constitutional form, the Royal Speech at the commencement of each Session. Once it was the King who spoke, now it is the Cabinet as the organ of the party who supports it; and it is rapidly becoming the practice for parties to outbid one another in the length of the tale of legislation to which they pledge themselves in successive Royal Speeches.

There is undoubted danger in looking upon politics as a deeply interesting game, a never-ending cricket-match between Blue and Yellow. The practice is yet more dangerous when the ever-accumulating stakes are legislative measures upon which the whole future of this country is risked; and the danger is peculiarly great under a constitutional system which does not provide for measures reforming the Constitution any different or more solemn procedure than that which is followed in ordinary legislation. Neither experience nor probability affords any ground for thinking that there may be an infinity of legislative innovation, at once safe and beneficent. On the contrary, it would be a safer conjecture that the possibilities of reform are strictly limited. The possibilities of heat,

it is said, reach 2,000 degrees of the Centigrade thermom-
eter; the possibilities of cold extend to about 300 degrees
below its zero; but all organic life in the world is only
possible through the accident that temperature in it
ranges between a maximum of 120 degrees and a minimum of a few degrees below zero of the Centigrade. For
all we know, a similarly narrow limitation may hold of
legislative changes in the structure of human society. We
can no more argue that, because some past reforms have
succeeded, all reforms will succeed, than we can argue
that, because the human body can bear a certain amount
of heat, it can bear an indefinite amount.

There are, however, many accidents of their history,
and particularly of their recent history, which blind Englishmen to the necessity of caution while they indulge in
the pastime of politics, particularly when the two sides
into which they divide themselves compete in legislative
innovation. We are singularly little sensible, as a nation,
of the extraordinary good luck which has befallen us
since the beginning of the century. Foreign observers (until perhaps the other day) were always dwelling on it, but
Englishmen, as a rule, do not notice it, or (it may be)
secretly believe that they deserve it. The fact is that, since
the century began, we have been victorious and prosper-
ous beyond all example. We have never lost a battle in
Europe or a square mile of territory; we have never taken
a ruinous step in foreign politics; we have never made an
irreparable mistake in legislation. If we compare our history with recent French history, there is nothing in it like
the disaster at Sedan or the loss of Alsace-Lorraine; nothing like the gratuitous quarrel with Germany about the

vacant Crown of Spain; nothing like the law of May 1850, which, by altering the suffrage, gave the great enemy of the Republic the opportunity for which he had been waiting. Yet, if we multiply occasions for such calamities, it is possible and even probable that they will occur; and it is useless to deny that, with the craving for political excitement which is growing on us every day, the chances of a great false step are growing also.

I do not think it likely to be denied, that the activity of popular government is more and more tending to exhibit itself in legislation, or that the materials for legislation are being constantly supplied in ever-increasing abundance through the competition of parties, or, lastly, that the keen interest which the community takes in looking on, as a body of spectators, at the various activities of popular government, is the chief reason of the general impression that ours is an Age of Progress, to be indefinitely continued. There are, however, other causes of this impression or belief, which are much less obvious and much less easily demonstrated to the ordinary English politician. At the head of them, are a group of words, phrases, maxims, and general propositions, which have their root in political theories, not indeed far removed from us by distance of time, but as much forgotten by the mass of mankind as if they had belonged to the remotest antiquity. How is one to convince the advanced English politician who announces with an air of pride that he is Radical, and indeed a Radical and something more, that he is calling himself by a name which he would never have had the courage to adopt, so deep was its disrepute, if Jeremy Bentham had not given it respectability by associating it with a particular theory of legislation and politics? How is one to persuade him, when he speaks of the Sovereign People, that he employs a combination of words which would never have occurred to his mind if in 1762 a French philosopher had not written a speculative essay on the origin of society, the formation of States, and the nature of government? Neither of these theories, the theory of Rousseau which starts from the assumed Natural Rights of Man, or the theory of Bentham which is based on the hypothetical Greatest Happiness principle, is now-a-days explicitly held by many people. The natural rights of man have indeed made their appearance in recent political discourse, producing much the same effect as if a professed lecturer on astronomy were to declare his belief in the Ptolemaic spheres and to call upon his audience to admire their music; but, of the two theories mentioned above, that of Rousseau which recognises these rights is much the most thoroughly forgotten. For the attempt to apply it led to terrible calamities, while the theory of Bentham has at present led to nothing worse than a certain amount of disappointment. How is it then that these wholly or partially exploded speculations still exercise a most real and practical influence on political thought? The fact is that political theories are endowed with the faculty possessed by the hero of the Border-ballad. When their legs are smitten off they fight upon their stumps. They produce a host of words, and of ideas associated with those words, which remain active and combatant after the parent speculation is mutilated or dead. Their posthumous influence often extends a good way beyond the domain of politics. It does not seem to

me a fantastic assertion that the ideas of one of the great
novelists of the last generation may be traced to Bentham,
and those of another to Rousseau. Dickens, who spent his
early manhood among the politicians of 1832 trained in
Bentham's school, hardly ever wrote a novel without attacking an abuse. The procedure of the Court of Chancery
and of the Ecclesiastical Courts, the delays of the Public
Offices, the costliness of divorce, the state of the dwell-
ings of the poor, and the condition of the cheap schools
in the North of England, furnished him with what he
seemed to consider, in all sincerity, the true moral of a
series of fictions. The opinions of Thackeray have a strong
resemblance to those to which Rousseau gave popularity.
It is a very just remark of Mill, that the attraction which
Nature and the State of Nature had for Rousseau may be
partly accounted for as a reaction against the excessive
admiration of civilisation and progress which took
possession of educated men during the earlier part of the
eighteenth century. Theoretically, at any rate, Thackeray
hated the artificialities of civilisation, and it must be
owned that some of his favourite personages have about
them something of Rousseau's natural man as he would
have shown himself if he had mixed in real life—something, that is, of the violent blackguard.

The influence which the political theory originating in
France and the political theory originating in England still
exercise over politics seems to me as certain as anything
in the history of thought can be. It is necessary to examine
these theories, because there is no other way of showing
the true value of the instruments, the derivative words
and derivative ideas, through which they act. I will take

first the famous constitutional theory of Rousseau, which, long unfamiliar or discredited in this country, is the fountain of many notions which have suddenly become popular and powerful among us. There is much difficulty in the attempt to place it in a clear light, for reasons well known to all who have given attention to the philosophy of the remarkable man who produced it. This philosophy is the most striking example extant of a confusion which may be detected in all corners of non-scientific modern thought, the confusion between what is and what ought to be, between what did as a fact occur and what under certain conditions would have occurred. The *Contrat Social,* which sets forth the political theory on which I am engaged, appears at first sight to give an historical account of the emergence of mankind from a State of Nature. But whether it is meant that mankind did emerge in this way, whether the writer believes that only a happily circumstanced part of the human race had this experience, or whether he thinks that Nature, a beneficent legislatress, intended all men to have it, but that her objects were defeated, it is quite impossible to say with any confidence. The language of Rousseau sometimes suggests that he meant his picture of early social transformations to be regarded as imaginary;[6] but

---

[6] "Comment ce changement s'est-il fait? Je l'ignore."—*Contrat Social,* chap. i. I have myself no doubt that very much of the influence of Rousseau over the men of his own generation, and of the next, arose from the belief widely spread among them that his account of natural and of early political society was literally true. There is a remarkable passage in the *Pensées* of Pascal (III. 8) which describes the powerful revolutionary effects which may be produced by contrasting an existing institution with some supposed "fundamental and primitive law" of the State. The reflection was obviously

nevertheless the account given of them is so precise, detailed, and logically built up, that it is quite inconceivable its author should not have intended it to express realities. This celebrated theory is briefly as follows. Rousseau, who in his earlier writings had strongly insisted on the disadvantages which man had sustained through the loss of his natural rights, begins the *Contrat Social* with the position that Man was originally in the State of Nature. So long as he remained in it, he was before all things free. But, in course of time, a point is reached at which the obstacles to his continuance in the natural condition become insuperable. Mankind then enter into the Social Compact under which the State, society, or community is formed. Their consent to make this compact must be unanimous; but the effect of its completion is the absolute alienation or surrender, by every individual human being, of his person and all his rights to the aggregate community.[7] The community then becomes the sovereign, the true and original Sovereign People, and it is an autocratic sovereign. It ought to maintain liberty and equality among its subjects, but only because the subjection of one individual to another is a loss of force to the State, and because there cannot be liberty without equality.[8] The

---

suggested by the sedition of the Fronde. The Parliament of Paris firmly believed in the "fundamental and primitive laws" of France; and, a century later, the disciples of Rousseau had exactly the same faith in the State of Nature and the Social Compact.

[7] "Le pacte social se réduit aux termes suivants: chacun de nous mit en commun sa personne et toute sa puissance sous la suprême direction de la volonté générale; et nous recevons encore chaque membre comme partie individuelle du tout."—*Contrat Social,* c. i. 6.

[8] *Contrat Social,* ii. 11.

collective despot cannot divide, or alienate, or delegate his power. The Government is his servant, and is merely the organ of correspondence between the sovereign and the people. No representation of the people is allowed. Rousseau abhorred the representative system; but periodical assemblies of the entire community are to be held, and two questions are to be submitted to them—whether it is the pleasure of the sovereign to maintain the present form of government—and whether the sovereign pleases to leave the administration of its affairs to the persons who now conduct it.[9] The autocracy of the aggregate community and the indivisibility, perpetuity, and incommunicable character of its power, are insisted upon in every part of the *Contrat Social* and in every form of words.

As is almost always the case with sweeping theories, portions of Rousseau's ideas may be discovered in the speculations of older writers. A part may be found, a century earlier, in the writings of Hobbes; another part in those of the nearly contemporary school of French Economists. But the theory, as he put it together, owes to him its extraordinary influence; and it is the undoubted parent of a host of phrases and associated notions which, after having long had currency in France and on the Continent, are beginning to have serious effect in this country, as the democratic element in its Constitution increases. From this origin sprang the People (with a capital P), the Sovereign People, the People the sole source

---

[9] *Contrat Social,* iii. 18. The decision is in this case to be by majority; Rousseau requires unanimity for the consent to enter into the Social Compact, but not otherwise.

of all legitimate power. From this came the subordination of Governments, not merely to electorates but to a vaguely defined multitude outside them, or to the still vaguer mastership of floating opinion. Hence began the limitation of legitimacy in governments to governments which approximate to democracy. A vastly more formidable conception bequeathed to us by Rousseau is that of the omnipotent democratic State rooted in natural right; the State which has at its absolute disposal everything which individual men value, their property, their persons, and their independence; the State which is bound to respect neither precedent nor prescription; the State which may make laws for its subjects ordaining what they shall drink or eat, and in what way they shall spend their earnings; the State which can confiscate all the land of the community, and which, if the effect on human motives is what it may be expected to be, may force us to labour on it when the older incentives to toil have disappeared. Nevertheless this political speculation, of which the remote and indirect consequences press us on all sides, is of all speculations the most baseless. The natural condition from which it starts is a simple figment of the imagination. So far as any research into the nature of primitive human society has any bearing on so mere a dream, all inquiry has dissipated it. The process by which Rousseau supposes communities of men to have been formed, or by which at all events he wishes us to assume that they were formed, is again a chimera. No general assertion as to the way in which human societies grew up is safe, but perhaps the safest of all is that none of them were formed in the way imagined by Rousseau.

The true relation of some parts of the theory to fact is very instructive. Some particles of Rousseau's thought may be discovered in the mental atmosphere of his time. "Natural law" and "natural rights" are phrases properly belonging to a theory not of politics, but of jurisprudence, which, originating with the Roman jurisconsults, had a great attraction for the lawyers of France. The despotic sovereign of the *Contrat Social,* the all-powerful community, is an inverted copy of the King of France invested with an authority claimed for him by his courtiers and by the more courtly of his lawyers, but denied to him by all the highest minds in the country, and specially by the great luminaries of the French Parliaments. The omnipotent democracy is the King-Proprietor, the lord of all men's fortunes and persons; but it is the French King turned upside down. The mass of natural rights absorbed by the sovereign community through the Social Compact is, again, nothing more than the old divine right of kings in a new dress. As for Rousseau's dislike of representative systems and his requirement that the entire community should meet periodically to exercise its sovereignty, his language in the *Contrat Social* suggests that he was led to these opinions by the example of the ancient tribal democracies. But at a later date he declared that he had the Constitution of Geneva before his mind;[10] and he cannot but have known that the exact method of government which he proposed still lived in the oldest cantons of Switzerland.

This denial to the collective community of all power

---

[10] *Lettres écrites de la Montagne,* part i., letter 6, p. 328.

of acting in its sovereign capacity through representatives is so formidable, as apparently to forbid any practical application of Rousseau's theory. Rousseau, indeed, expressly says[11] that his principles apply to small communities only, hinting at the same time that they may be adapted to States having a large territory by a system of confederation; and in this hint we may suspect that we have the germ of the opinion, which has become an article of faith in modern Continental Radicalism, that freedom is best secured by breaking up great commonwealths into small self-governing communes. But the time was not ripe for such a doctrine at the end of the last century; and real vitality was for the first time given to the speculation of Rousseau by that pamphlet of Siéyès, *Qu'est-ce que le Tiers État?* which did so much to determine the early stages of the French Revolution. As even the famous first page[12] of this pamphlet is often misquoted, what follows it is not perhaps always carefully read, and it may have escaped notice that much of it[13] simply reproduces the theory of Rousseau. But then Siéyès reproduces this theory with a difference. The most important claim which he advanced, and which he succeeded in making good, was that the Three Orders should sit together and form a National Assembly. The argument by which he reaches

---

[11] *Contrat Social,* iii. 15.

[12] The first page runs: "1. Qu'est-ce que le Tiers État?—Tout. 2. Qu'a-t-il été jusqu'à présent dans l'ordre politique?—Rien. 3. Que demande-t-il?—À être quelque chose." It is misquoted by Alison, *History of Europe during the French Revolution,* vol. i. c. iii. p. 453.

[13] The argument fills the long chapter v. The edition before me is the third, published in 1789.

this conclusion is substantially that of the *Contrat Social.* With Siéyès, as with Rousseau, man begins in the natural condition; he enters society by a social compact; and by virtue of this compact an all-powerful community is formed. But then Siéyès had not the objection of Rousseau to representation, which indeed was one of his favourite subjects of speculation during life. He allows the community to make a large preliminary delegation of its powers by representation. Thus is formed the class of representative bodies to which the future National Assembly of France was to belong. Siéyès calls them *extraordinary,* and describes them as exercising their will like men in a state of nature, as standing in place of the nation, as incapable of being tied down to any particular decision or line of legislation. *Ordinary* representative bodies are, on the other hand, legislatures deriving their powers from a Constitution which the extraordinary Assembly has formed and strictly confined to the exercise of these powers. The extraordinary assembly is thus the sovereign community of Rousseau; the ordinary assembly is his government. To the first class belong those despotic bodies which, under the name of National Assembly or Convention, have four times governed France, never successfully and sometimes disastrously. To the second belong the Legislative Assemblies and Chambers of Deputies so often overthrown by revolution.

The other theory, from which a number of political phrases and political ideas now circulating among us have descended, is of English origin, and had Jeremy Bentham for its author. Its contribution to this currency is at this moment smaller than that which may be traced to a

French source in the *Contrat Social,* but it was at one time
much larger. It must be carefully borne in mind that during the earlier and greater part of his long life Bentham
was not a reformer of Constitutions, but a reformer of
Law. He was the first Englishman to see clearly how the
legislative powers of the State, very sparingly employed
for this object before, could be used to rearrange and
reconstruct civil jurisprudence and adapt it to its professed ends. He became a Radical Reformer—an expression to which, as I said before, he gave a new respectability—through sheer despair.[14] The British Constitution
in his day might no doubt have been improved in many
of its parts, but, in his impatience of delay in legislative
reforms, he attributed to inherent defects in the Constitution obstructions which were mainly owing to the effects
produced on the entire national mind by detestation of
principles, strongly condemned by himself, which had
brought on France the Reign of Terror and on the entire
Continent the military despotism of Napoleon Bonaparte.
Superficially, the ideal political system for which he argued in a series of pamphlets has not a little resemblance
to that of Rousseau and Siéyès. There was to be a single-
chambered democracy, one all-powerful representative
assembly, with powers unrestricted theoretically, but
with its action facilitated and guided by a strange and
complex apparatus of subordinate institutions.[15] The real
difference between his plans and those of the French
theorist lay in their philosophical justification. The sys-

---

[14] See the Introduction to his plan of Parliamentary Reform. *Works,* iii. 436.
[15] *Constitutional Code. Works,* ix. 1.

tem of Rousseau was based on the pretended Natural Rights of men, and it owes to this basis a hold on weaker and less instructed minds, which is rather increasing than diminishing. But Bentham utterly repudiated those Natural Rights, and denounced the conception of them as absurd and anarchical. During the first or law-reforming period of his life, which lasted till he was more than sixty years old, he had firmly grasped the "greatest happiness of the greatest number" (a form of words found in Beccaria) as the proper standard of legislative reform; but, observing the close association of law with morals, he had made the bolder attempt to reform moral ideas on the same principle, and by a sort of legislation to force men to think and feel, as well as to act, in conformity with his standard. As the great war proceeded, the time became more and more unfavourable for Bentham's experiment, and finally he himself declared that the cause of reform was lost on the plains of Waterloo. It was then that he began his attack on the British Constitution, and published his proposals for reconstructing it from base to apex. As the classes which it placed in power refused to recognise or promote the greatest happiness of the greatest number, he proposed to displace them and to hand over all political authority to the greatest number itself. It must necessarily follow his standard, he argued; every man and every number of men seeks its own happiness, and the greatest number armed with legislative power must legislate for its own happiness. This reasoning had great effect on some of the most powerful minds of Bentham's day. His disciples—Grote, the two Mills, Molesworth, the two Austins, and Roebuck—did really do much to transform the British Constitution. Some of them, however, lived long enough to be disenchanted by the results;[16] and, I have attempted to show in a former Essay, many of these results would have met with the deepest disapproval from Bentham himself. The truth is, there was a serious gap in his reasoning. Little can be said against "the greatest happiness of the greatest number" as a standard of legislation, and indeed it is the only standard which the legislative power, when once called into action, can possibly follow. It is inconceivable that any legislator should deliberately propose or pass a measure intended to diminish the happiness of the majority of the citizens. But when this multitudinous majority is called to the Government for the purpose of promoting its own happiness, it now becomes evident that, independently of the enormous difficulty of obtaining any conclusion from a multitude of men, there is no security that this multitude will know what its own happiness is, or how it can be promoted. On this point it must be owned that Rousseau shows himself wiser than Bentham. He claimed for the entire community that it should be

---

[16] I quote the following passage from the Preface to John Austin's *Plea for the Constitution*. "In the course of the following Essay I have advanced opinions which are now unpopular, and which may possibly expose me to some obloquy, though I well remember the time (for I was then a Radical) when the so-called Liberal opinions which are now predominant exposed the few who professed them to political and social proscription. I have said that the bulk of the working-classes are not yet qualified for political power. . . . I have said this because I think so. I am no worshipper of the great and rich, and have no fancy for their style of living. I am by origin, and by my strongest sympathies, a man of the people; and I have never desired, for a single moment, to ascend from the modest station which I have always occupied."

sovereign and that it should exercise its sovereignty in the plenitude of power, because these were its Natural Rights; but, though he claimed for it that it should be all-powerful, he did not claim that it was all-wise, for he knew that it was not. The People, he said, always meant well; but it does not always judge well.

> Comment une multitude aveugle, qui souvent ne sait ce qu'elle veut, parce qu'elle sait rarement ce qui lui est bon, exécuterait-elle d'elle-même une entreprise aussi grande, aussi difficile, qu'un système de législation? De lui-même le peuple veut toujours le bien, mais de lui-même il ne le voit pas toujours. La volonté générale est toujours droite, mais le jugement qui la guide n'est pas toujours éclairé.[17]

Rousseau was led by these misgivings almost to doubt the practical possibility of wise legislation by his ideal democracy. He seems to have thought that the legislator who could properly guide the people in the exercise of their sovereign powers would only appear at long intervals, and must virtually be semi-divine. In connection with these ideas, he made a prediction which has contributed nearly as much to his fame as any of his social and political speculations. Sharing the general interest and sympathy which the gallant struggle of the Corsicans for independence had excited in his day, he persuaded himself that the ideal legislator would most probably arise in Corsica. "J'ai quelque pressentiment," he writes, "qu'un jour, cette petite île étonnera l'Europe." The prophecy has been repeatedly taken to mean that Rousseau foresaw the birth in Corsica, seven years later, of a

---

[17] *Contrat Social,* ii. 6. The latter part of this chapter is replete with good sense.

military genius after whom the Code Civil of France would be named.

One further remark, not perhaps at first sight obvious, ought to be made of these political theories of Rousseau and Bentham which contribute so largely to the mental stock of the classes now rising to power in Europe. These theories were, in their origin, theories not of constitutional reform, but of law-reform. It is unnecessary to give new proof of this assertion as respects Bentham. But it is also true of Rousseau. The conceptions of Nature, of Natural Law, and of Natural Right, which prompted and shaped his political speculations, are first found in the language of the Roman lawyers. It is more than doubtful whether these illustrious men ever believed in the State of Nature as a reality, but they seem to have thought that, under all the perverse technicalities of ancient law, there lay a simple and symmetrical system of rules which were in some sense those of Nature. Their natural law was, for all practical purposes, simple or simplified law. This view, with all its philosophical defects, led to a great simplification of law both in the Roman State and in modern Europe, and indeed was the chief source of law-reform until the system of Bentham, which also aimed at the simplification of law, made its appearance. But the undoubted descent both of the French and the English political theory from theories of law-reform points to a serious weakness in them. That because you can successfully reform jurisprudence on certain principles, you can successfully reform Constitutions on the same principles, is not a safe inference. In the first place, the simplification of civil law, its disentanglement from idle forms, technicalities, obscurities, and illogicalities, can scarcely be other than a beneficial process. It may indeed lead to disappointment. Bentham thought that, if law were reformed on his principles, litigation would be easy, cheap, and expeditious; yet, now that nearly all his proposals have been adopted, the removal of legal difficulties seems to have brought into still greater nakedness the difficulties of questions of fact. But, though the simplification of law may lead to disappointment, it can scarcely lead to danger. It is, however, idle to conceal from oneself that the simplification of political institutions leads straight to absolutism, the absolutism not of an expert judge, but of a single man or of a multitude striving to act as if it were a single man. The illogicalities swept away in the process may really be buttresses which helped to support the vast burden of government, or checks which mitigated the consequences of the autocrat's undeniable fallibility. Again, a mistake in law-reform is of small importance. It mainly affects a class of whose grievances, I may observe, Bentham had far too exalted a notion, the small part of the community which actually "goes to law." If committed, it can be corrected with comparative ease. But a mistake in constitutional innovation directly affects the entire community and every part of it. It may be fraught with calamity or ruin, public or private. And correction is virtually impossible. It is practically taken for granted among us, that all constitutional changes are final and must be submitted to, whatever their consequences. Doubtless this assumption arises from a general belief that, in these matters, we are propelled by an irresistible force on a definite path towards an unavoidable end—towards Democracy, as towards Death.

If there be force in the considerations which I have urged, the ideas current among us as to the Age of Progress through which we are supposed to be passing will stand in need of a great deal of modification. In one important particular, they will have to be exactly reversed. The natural condition of mankind (if that word "natural" is used) is not the progressive condition. It is a condition not of changeableness but of unchangeableness. The immobility of society is the rule; its mobility is the exception. The toleration of change and the belief in its advantages are still confined to the smallest portion of the human race, and even with that portion they are extremely modern. They are not much more than a century old on the Continent of Europe; and not much more than half a century old in Great Britain. When they are found, the sort of change which they contemplate is of a highly special kind, being exclusively political change. The process is familiar enough to Englishmen. A number of persons, often a small minority, obtain the ear of the governing part of the community, and persuade it to force the entire community to conform itself to their ideas. Doubtless there is a general submission to this process, and an impression even among those who dislike it that it will go very far. But when the causes of this state of feeling are examined, they appear to arise in a very small degree from intelligent conviction, but to a very great extent from the remote effects of words and notions derived from broken-down political theories. If this be the truth, or even an approximation to the truth, it suggests some very simple and obvious inferences. If modern society be not essentially and normally changeable, the attempt to conduct it safely through the unusual and exceptional process of change is not easy but extremely difficult. What is easy to a man is that which has come to him through a long-inherited experience, like walking or using his fingers; what is difficult to him is that in which such experience gives him little guidance or none at all, like riding or skating. It is extremely probable that the Darwinian rule, "small changes benefit the organism," holds good of communities of men, but a sudden sweeping political reform constantly places the community in the position of an individual who should mount a horse solely on the strength of his studies in a work on horsemanship.

These conclusions, which I venture to think are conclusions of common sense, go a long way to explain a series of facts which at first sight are not quite intelligible. What is the reason of the advantage which historical Constitutions, Constitutions gradually developed through the accumulation of experience, appear as a fact to enjoy over *à priori* Constitutions, Constitutions founded on speculative assumptions remote from experience? That the advantage exists, will hardly be denied by any educated Englishman. With Conservatives this is of course an axiom, but there are few really eminent men on the opposite side who do not from time to time betray the same opinion, especially in presence of a catastrophe suffered by some Constitution of the last-mentioned type. Not many persons in the last century could have divined from the previous opinions of Edmund Burke the real substructure of his political creed, or did in fact suspect it till it was uncovered by the early and comparatively slight miscarriage of French revolutionary institutions. A great disillusion has always seemed to me to separate the "Thoughts on the Present Discontents in 1770" and the "Speech on American Taxation in 1774" from the magnificent panegyric on the British Constitution in 1790.

> Our political system is placed in a just correspondence and symmetry with the order of the world and with the mode of existence decreed to a permanent body composed of transitory parts; wherein, by the disposition of a stupendous wisdom, moulding together the great mysterious incorporation of the human race, the whole, at one time, is never old, or middle-aged, or young, but in a condition of unchangeable constancy moves on through the varied tenour of perpetual decay, fall, renovation, and progression. Thus, in preserving that method of nature in the conduct of the State, in what we improve we are never wholly new; in what we retain, we are never wholly obsolete.[18]

Macaulay, again, happened to have to close his account of the Revolution of 1688 just when a new French experiment in *à priori* Constitution-building had spread confusion through the Continent of Europe, and his picture of the events which gave birth to the party that had a monopoly of his admiration would almost rob them of their historical name of "Revolution Whigs," which he nevertheless claimed for them.

> As our Revolution was a vindication of ancient rights, so it was conducted with strict attention to ancient formalities. In almost every word and act may be discerned a profound reverence for the Past. The Estates of the Realm deliberated in the old halls and according to the old rules. . . . The speeches pre-

---

[18] Burke, *Reflections on the Revolution in France*, vol. v. of *Works*, p. 70.

sent an almost ludicrous contrast to the revolutionary oratory
of every other country. Both the English parties agreed in treat-
ing with solemn respect the ancient constitutional traditions of
the State. The only question was, in what sense these traditions
were to be understood. The assertors of liberty said nothing
about the natural equality of men and the inalienable sovereignty of the people, about Harmodius or Timoleon, Brutus the
elder or Brutus the younger. When they are told that, by the
English law, the Crown, at the moment of a demise, must de-
scend to the next heir, they answered that, by the English law,
a living man could have no heir. When they were told that there
was no precedent for declaring the throne vacant, they produced
from among the records in the Tower a roll of parchment, near
three hundred years old, on which, in quaint characters and
barbarous Latin, it was recorded that the Estates of the Realm
had declared vacant the throne of a perfidious and tyrannical
Plantagenet. When at length the dispute had been accommodated, the new sovereigns were proclaimed with the old pa-
geantry. All the fantastic pomp of heraldry was there, Claren-
cieux and Norroy, Portcullis and Rouge Dragon, the trumpets,
the banners, the grotesque coats embroidered with lions and
lilies. The title of King of France, assumed by the conqueror of
Cressy, was not omitted in the royal style. To us, who have lived
in the year 1848, it may seem almost an abuse of terms to call
a proceeding, conducted with so much deliberation, with so
much sobriety, and with such minute attention to prescriptive
etiquette, by the terrible name of Revolution.[19]

In the light of historical facts neither the rhetoric of
Burke nor the rhetoric of Macaulay is unjust. I will not
undertake to hold the balance of success or failure among
the 350 Constitutions which a modern writer[20] declares
to have come into existence since the beginning of this
century; but if we take our standing ground at the end

---

[19] Macaulay, *History of England,* chap. x. *Works,* ii. 395, 396.
[20] Lieber, *Civil Liberty and Self-government,* Introduction.

of the century preceding, when *à priori* Constitutions first appeared, we find it certain that among all historical Constitutions there have been no failures so great and terrible as those of Constitutions of the other class. There have been oppressive Constitutions of the historical type; there have been Constitutions which mischievously obstructed the path of improvement; but with these there has been nothing like the disastrous course and end of the three Constitutions which announce their character by beginning with a Declaration of the Rights of Man, the French semi-monarchical Constitution of 1791, the French Republican Constitution of 1793, and the French Republican-Directorial Constitution of 1795. Nor has any historical Constitution had the ludicrous fate of the Constitution of December 1799, which came from the hands of Siéyès a marvel of balanced powers, and became by a single transposition the charter of a pure despotism. All this, however, is extremely intelligible, if human nature has always a very limited capacity, as in general it has very slight taste, for adjusting itself to new conditions. The utmost it can do is to select parts of its experience and apply them tentatively to these conditions; and this process is always awkward and often dangerous. A community with a new *à priori* political constitution is at best in the disagreeable position of a British traveller whom a hospitable Chinese entertainer has constrained to eat a dinner with chopsticks. Let the new institutions be extraordinarily wide of experience, and inconvenience becomes imminent peril. The body-politic is in that case like the body-natural transported to a new climate, unaccustomed food, and strange surroundings. Sometimes it perishes altogether. Sometimes the most unexpected parts of its organisation develop themselves at the expense of others; and when the ingenious legislator had counted on producing a nation of self-denying and somewhat sentimental patriots, he finds that he has created a people of Jacobins or a people of slaves.

It is in a high degree likely that the British Parliament and the British electorate will soon have to consider which of these two principles, assumption or experience, they will apply to a great and ancient institution, of all our institutions the one which on the whole has departed least from its original form. I put aside the question which of them it is that has been applied to the constituent body of the House of Commons. That is over, and its consequences, in Homeric phrase, "lie upon the knees of the gods." But, surprising as was the way in which the question of Franchise and Redistribution ended, and in which the question of reconstructing the House of Lords, which had been mixed up with it, fell suddenly into the background, no observant man can doubt that the last question will before long press again for attention. The very variety of opinion which, as I pointed out in the last Essay, prevails among politicians of every party colour as to the mode in which the legal power of the House of Lords should be exercised, is an earnest of a controversy soon to be revived; and indeed the mere demand for continuous important legislation will soon force into notice so great an addition to the supply as the reform of the Upper House. The quarrel which raged for a while on platforms and in the newspapers threw up a great number of suggestions for change, out of which very few were

worthy of consideration. They varied from a proposal to
dispense altogether with a Second Chamber to proposals
for a Chamber of Peers nominated for life; proposals for
empowering the Crown to select a limited number of
Peers out of the present body for service in each Parliament; proposals for giving to the entire present House of
Lords the right to elect this limited number; proposals for
a Second Chamber of experienced executive officers, and
proposals for a Senate to which the Local Government
Circles (as yet unformed) should furnish constituencies.
But, amid these loose guesses at a reasonable solution of
a great question, there was much language employed
which seemed to me to betray serious misconception of
the nature of a Second or Upper House, and these opinions merit some consideration.

Let me take first the most trenchant of the proposals
recently before the country, the scheme for governing
through a Parliament consisting of a single Chamber. This
plan was advocated by Mr. J. S. Mill in one of his later
writings, but it is just to him to bear in mind that in the
single Chamber he proposed there was to be a minutely
accurate representation of minorities. This condition was
dropped in the late controversy, and it was thought
enough to quote the well-known epigram of Siéyès on
the subject of Second Chambers. "If," it runs, "a Second
Chamber dissents from the First, it is mischievous; if it
agrees, it is superfluous." It has perhaps escaped notice
that this saying is a conscious or unconscious parody of
that reply of the Caliph Omar about the books of the
Alexandrian Library which caused them to be burnt. "If
the books," said the Commander of the Faithful to his

lieutenant, "differ from the book of the Prophet, they are impious; if they agree, they are useless." The reasoning is precisely the same in both cases, and starts from the same assumption. It takes for granted that a particular utterance is divine. If the Koran is the inspired and exclusive word of God, Omar was right; if Vox Populi, Vox Dei, expresses a truth, Siéyès was right. If the decisions of the community, conveyed through one particular organ, are not only imperative but all-wise, a Second Chamber is a superfluity or an impertinence. There is no question that the generality of First Chambers, or popularly elected Houses, do make the assumption on which this argument rests. They do not now-a-days rest their claim to authority on the English theory of the advantages of a balance of the historical elements in a given society. They do not appeal to the wise deduction from experience, as old as Aristotle, which no student of constitutional history will deny, that the best Constitutions are those in which there is a large popular element. It is a singular proof of the widespread influence of the speculations of Rousseau that, although very few First Chambers really represent the entire community (indeed, there is no agreement as to what the entire community is, and nobody is quite sure how it can be represented), nevertheless in Europe they almost invariably claim to reflect it, and, as a consequence, they assume an air of divinity which, if it rightfully belonged to them, would be fatal to all argument for a Second Chamber.

There appears to me to be no escaping from the fact that all such institutions as a Senate, a House of Peers, or a Second Chamber, are founded on a denial or a doubt of the proposition that the voice of the people is the voice of God. They express the revolt of a great mass of human common sense against it. They are the fruit of the agnosticism of the political understanding. Their authors and advocates do not assert that the decisions of a popularly elected Chamber are always or generally wrong. These decisions are very often right. But it is impossible to be sure that they are right. And the more the difficulties of multitudinous government are probed, and the more carefully the influences acting upon it are examined, the stronger grows the doubt of the infallibility of popularly elected legislatures. What, then, is expected from a well-constituted Second Chamber is not a rival infallibility, but an additional security. It is hardly too much to say that, in this view, almost any Second Chamber is better than none. No such Chamber can be so completely un-satisfactory that its concurrence does not add some weight to a presumption that the First Chamber is in the right; but doubtless Upper Houses may be so constituted, and their discussions so conducted, that their concurrence would render this presumption virtually conclusive. The conception of an Upper House as a mere revising body, trusted with the privilege of dotting i's and crossing t's in measures sent up by the other Chamber, seems to me as irrational as it is poor. What is wanted from an Upper House is the security of its concurrence, after full exami-nation of the measure concurred in.

It requires some attention to facts to see how widely spread is the misgiving as to the absolute wisdom of popularly elected Chambers. I will not stop to examine the American phenomena of this class, but will merely

observe in passing, that the one thoroughly successful
institution which has been established since the tide of
modern democracy began to run, is a Second Chamber,
the American Senate. On the Continent of Europe there
are no States without Second Chambers, except three—
Greece, Serbia, and Bulgaria—all resembling one another
in having long been portions of the Turkish Empire, and
in being now very greatly under the influence of the
Russian Government. Russia has not, Turkey never had,
any true aristocracy, any "root of gentlemen," to repeat
Bacon's expression; and we shall see presently that the
framers of Constitutions, in their search for materials of
a Second Chamber other than the ordinary forms of
popular election, have constantly had to build, at all
events partially, on the foundation of an aristocracy. But,
with the exception of the three communities just mentioned, all the European States have Second Chambers,
varying from that of Norway, where, after a single general election, a certain number of the deputies returned
are told off to make an Upper House, to the ultra-aris-
tocratic House of Magnates established from the earliest time[21] under the ancient Hungarian Constitution.
Hereditary Peers, generally mixed with Life Peers and
elective Peers, are still common in the Second Chambers
of the Continent; they are found in Cis-Leithan Austria,
in Prussia, in Bavaria, in many of the smaller German
States, in Spain, and in Portugal. There is much reason
to believe that the British House of Lords would have

---

[21] Since this essay appeared in its first form, the House of Magnates has
undergone a reform which still leaves it a highly aristocratic body.

been exclusively, or at all events much more extensively, copied in the Constitutions of the Continent, but for one remarkable difficulty. This is not in the least any dislike or distrust of the hereditary principle, but the extreme numerousness of the nobility in most Continental societies, and the consequent difficulty of selecting a portion of them to be exclusively privileged. Siéyès, in his famous pamphlet, observes that in 1789 the higher French aristocracy was eager[22] to have a House of Lords engrafted on the new French Constitution; and this ambition, as Burke noticed, was the secret of the fervour—the suicidal fervour, as it afterwards turned out—with which a certain number of the noblest French families threw in their lot with the Revolutionary movement. Siéyès, however, pointed out the fatal obstacle to these hopes. It was the number and the theoretical equality of the nobles. His calculation was that, in all France, there were no less than 110,000 noblemen; there were 10,000 in Brittany alone. The proportions which this difficulty sometimes still assumes on the Continent may be inferred from one curious instance. The combined Parliament of the two small States called respectively Mecklenburg-Schwerin and Mecklenburg-Strelitz in a mediæval Diet, very slightly changed. It now consists of 731 members, of whom 684 are persons of knightly rank, holding land by knightly tenure. As a rule, however, this numerousness of the nobility causes the privilege of sitting in the Upper House

---

[22] Siéyès. *Qu'est-ce que le Tiers Etat?* chap. iv. "Tout ce qui tient aux quatre cents familles les plus distinguées soupire après l'établissement d'une Chambre Haute, semblable à celle d'Angleterre."

to be confined to comparatively few Peers of very high and universally acknowledged rank, and hereditary Peers are seldom found without an intermixture of Life Peers. Life Peers also occur by themselves, but the Crown is generally directed by the Constitution to select them from certain classes of distinguished men. The best example of an Upper House formed by this method is the Italian Senate.

In the French Republic and in most of the Monarchical European States, elective Senators are found, either by themselves or together with Life Senators or Hereditary Peers. The mode of choosing them deserves careful attention. Sometimes the Senatorial electorate is different from that which chooses the Lower House; where, for instance, there is a property qualification, it is often higher in the case of Senatorial electors than in the case of electors for a Chamber of Deputies. More often, however, as in the case of France, Sweden, Denmark, the Netherlands, and Belgium, the elective Senators are chosen by an electorate which in principle is the same with that which returns the other Chamber. But then the electors are differently grouped. Provinces, cities, communes, elect the Senators; while the Deputies are assumed to be chosen by the nation at large. Nothing brings out so clearly as does this class of contrivances a fundamental doubt afflicting the whole Democratic theory. It is taken for granted that a popular electorate will be animated by a different spirit according as it is grouped; but why should there be any connection between the grouping of the People and the Voice of the People? The truth is, that as soon as we begin to reflect seriously on modes of practically applying the democratic principle, we find that some vital preliminary questions have never been settled. Granting that the People is entitled of right to govern, how is it to give its decisions and orders? Rousseau answers that all the people must meet periodically in assembly. Siéyès replies that it may speak through representatives, but he spent a life and displayed marvels of ingenuity in devising systems of representation; and the difficulties which he never succeeded in solving still perplex the absolute theorist. Vox Populi may be Vox Dei, but very little attention shows that there never has been any agreement as to what Vox means or as to what Populus means. Is the voice of the People the voice which speaks through *scrutin d'arrondissement* or through *scrutin de liste,* by Plébiscite or by tumultuary assembly? Is it a sound in which the note struck by minorities is entirely silent? Is the People which speaks, the People according to household suffrage, or the People according to universal suffrage, the People with all the women excluded from it, or the People, men, women, and children together, assembling casually in voluntary meeting? None of these questions has been settled; some have hardly been thought about. In reality, the devotee of Democracy is much in the same position as the Greeks with their oracles. All agreed that the voice of an oracle was the voice of a god; but everybody allowed that when he spoke he was not as intelligible as might be desired, and nobody was quite sure whether it was safer to go to Delphi or to Dodona.

It is needless to say that none of these difficulties embarrass the saner political theorist who holds that, in secular matters, it is better to walk by sight than by faith.

As regards popularly elected Chambers, he will be satisfied that, to Englishmen as to Greeks, experience has
shown the best Constitutions to be those in which the
popular element is large; and he will readily admit that,
as the structure of each society of men slowly alters, it
is well to alter and amend the organisation by which this
element makes itself felt. But, as regards the far more
difficult undertaking of reconstructing an Upper House,
he will hope that it will fall into the hands of men who
have thoroughly brought home to themselves the truth,
that only two Second Chambers have as yet had any
duration to speak of—the American Senate, with all its
success a creation of yesterday, and the ancient English
House of Lords. It is very difficult to obtain from the
younger institution any lessons which can be of use in
the reconstruction of the older. The Senate of the United
States is, in strictness, no more a democratic institution
than the House of Lords. As I shall point out in the
following Essay, it is founded on inequality of representation, not on equality. But then, on the other hand, the
several States which depute the senators to Washington
are for the most part of older origin than the Federal
Union; they still retain some portion of sovereignty; and
thus no artificial Local Government circles which may be
created in this country will have more than a superficial
resemblance to them. It is only, I am persuaded, by careful
examination of infirmities which experience has shown
to exist in the House of Lords, and by careful consideration of doubts which have actually arisen as to the principles proper for it to follow in exercising its legal powers,
that hints of any kind can be gathered respecting its pos-

sible improvement. The most competent reformers of the House of Lords will probably be those who understand it from belonging to it; and doubtless there are times when the maxim of Portalis applies, "Il faut innover quand la plus funeste de toutes les innovations serait de ne point innover." Meantime, there does not seem to me to be anything in the thought and tendencies of our day which lends support to the vague propositions—powerful, I admit, through their very vagueness—which suggest that the improvement of the House of Lords is a desperate undertaking. One hears it said that the House of Lords consists of great landowners, and that the history of landed property in great masses is nearly ended; that the privileges of the Peers are hereditary, and that an hereditary right to share in government is absurd; and that the age of aristocracies and of aristocratic ascendency is gone for ever. These are very broad generalities, against which may be set off other generalities, perhaps equally broad, but much better supported by experience and observation. It certainly does appear that, for the moment, landed property is seriously threatened. Yet it demands but little penetration of mind to see that most of the current objections to it are objections to all private property, and there may again be a time when it is recognised that the possession of a great estate, as is natural in a form of ownership probably descended from a form of sovereignty,[23] implies more administrative power and kindlier

---

[23] I have discussed this point in an earlier work, *Early History of Institutions,* pp. 115 *et seq.* and pp. 130 *et seq.*

relations with other classes having subordinate interests than almost any other kind of superiority founded on wealth. The assertion of the inherent absurdity of an hereditary legislature will seem itself absurd to those who can follow the course of scientific thought in our day. Under all systems of government, under Monarchy, Aristocracy, and Democracy alike, it is a mere chance whether the individual called to the direction of public affairs will be qualified for the undertaking; but the chance of his competence, so far from being less under Aristocracy than under the other two systems, is distinctly greater. If the qualities proper for the conduct of government can be secured in a limited class or body of men, there is a strong probability that they will be transmitted to the corresponding class in the next generation, although no assertion be possible as to individuals. Whether—and this is the last objection—the age of aristocracies be over, I cannot take upon myself to say. I have sometimes thought it one of the chief drawbacks on modern democracy that, while it gives birth to despotism with the greatest facility, it does not seem to be capable of producing aristocracy, though from that form of political and social ascendency all improvement has hitherto sprung. But some of the keenest observers of democratic society in our day do not share this opinion. Noticing that the modern movement towards democracy is coupled with a movement towards scientific perfection, they appear to be persuaded that the world will some day fall under intellectual aristocracies. Society is to become the Church of a sort of political Calvinism, in which the Elect are to be the men with exceptional brains. This seems to be the view suggested

by French democratic society to M. Ernest Renan.[24]
Whether such an aristocracy, if it wielded all the power
which the command of all scientific results placed in its
hands, would be exactly beneficent, may possibly be
doubted. The faults to which the older privileged orders
are liable are plain enough and at times very serious. They
are in some characters idleness, luxuriousness, insolence,
and frivolity; in others, and more particularly in our day,
they are timidity, distrust of the permanence of anything
ancient and great, and (what is worse) a belief that no
reputation can be made by a member of an ancient and
great institution except by helping to pull it down. But,
assuming the utmost indulgence in these faults, I may be
permitted to doubt whether mankind would derive un-
mixed advantage from putting in their place an ascetic
aristocracy of men of science, with intellects perfected by
unremitting exercise, absolutely confident in themselves
and absolutely sure of their conclusions. The question,
however, will not long or deeply trouble those who, like
me, have the strongest suspicion that, if there really arise
a conflict between Democracy and Science, Democracy,

---

[24] Renan, *Dialogues Philosophiques.* Third Dialogue. A younger writer, M. Paul
Bourget, expresses himself as follows in a remarkable book called *Essais de
Psychologie contemporaine.* "Il est possible, en effet, qu'une divergence éclate entre
ces deux grandes forces des sociétés modernes: la démocratic et la science.
Il est certain que la première tend de plus en plus à niveler, tandis que la
seconde tend de plus en plus à créer des différences. 'Savoir, c'est pouvoir,'
disait le philosophe de l'induction, savoir dix fois plus qu'un autre homme,
c'est pouvoir dix fois ce qu'il peut, et comme la chimère d'une instruction
également répartie sur tous les individus est, sans aucun doute, irréalisable,
par suite de l'inégalité des intelligences, l'antinomie se manifestera de plus
en plus entre les tendances de la démocratie et les résultats sociaux de la
science" (pp. 106, 107).

which is already taking precautions against the enemy, will certainly win.

Note A[25]

"Mr. Tylor has justly observed that the true lesson of the new science of Comparative Mythology is the barrenness in primitive times of the faculty which we most associate with mental fertility, the Imagination. Comparative Jurisprudence, as might be expected from the natural stability of law and custom, yet more strongly suggests the same inference, and points to the fewness of ideas and the slowness of additions to the mental stock as among the most general characteristics of mankind in its infancy.

"The fact that the generation of new ideas does not proceed in all states of society as rapidly as in that to which we belong, is only not familiar to us through our inveterate habit of confining our observation of human nature to a small portion of its phenomena. When we undertake to examine it, we are very apt to look exclusively at a pãrt of Western Europe and perhaps of the American Continent. We constantly leave aside India, China, and the whole Mahometan East. This limitation of our field of vision is perfectly justifiable when we are occupied with the investigation of the laws of Progress. Progress is, in fact, the same thing as the continued production of new ideas, and we can only discover the law of this production by examining sequences of ideas where they are frequent and of considerable length. But the

---

[25] This Note is taken from my *Early History of Institutions*, pp. 225–230.

primitive condition of the progressive societies is best ascertained from the observable condition of those which are non-progressive; and thus we leave a serious gap in our knowledge when we put aside the mental state of the millions upon millions of men who fill what we vaguely call the East as a phenomenon of little interest and of no instructiveness. The fact is not unknown to most of us that, among these multitudes, Literature, Religion, and Art—or what corresponds to them—move always within a distinctly drawn circle of unchanging notions; but the fact that this condition of thought is rather the infancy of the human mind prolonged than a different maturity from the most familiar to us, is very seldom brought home to us with a clearness rendering it fruitful of instruction.

"I do not, indeed, deny that the difference between the East and the West, in respect of the different speed at which new ideas are produced, is only a difference of degree. There were new ideas produced in India even during the disastrous period just before the English entered it, and in the earlier ages this production must have been rapid. There must have been a series of ages during which the progress of China was very steadily maintained, and doubtless our assumption of the absolute immobility of the Chinese and other societies is in part the expression of our ignorance. Conversely, I question whether new ideas come into being in the West as rapidly as modern literature and conversation sometimes suggest. It cannot, indeed, be doubted that causes, unknown to the ancient world, lead among us to the multiplication of ideas. Among them are the never-ceasing discovery of new facts of nature, inventions changing the circumstances and material conditions of life, and new rules of social conduct; the chief of this last class, and certainly the most powerful in the domain of law proper, I take to be the famous maxim that all institutions should be adapted to produce the greatest happiness of the greatest number. Nevertheless, there are not a few signs that even conscious efforts to increase the number of ideas have a very limited success. Look at Poetry and Fiction. From time to time one mind endowed with the assemblage of qualities called genius makes a great and sudden addition to the combinations of thought, word, and sound which it is the province of those arts to produce; yet as suddenly, after one or a few such efforts, the productive activity of both branches of invention ceases, and they settle down into imitativeness for perhaps a century at a time. An humbler example may be sought in rules of social habit. We speak of the caprices of Fashion; yet, on examining them historically, we find them singularly limited, so much so, that we are sometimes tempted to regard Fashion as passing through cycles of form ever repeating themselves. There are, in fact, more natural limitations on the fertility of intellect than we always admit to ourselves, and these, reflected in bodies of men, translate themselves into that weariness of novelty which seems at intervals to overtake whole Western societies, including minds of every degree of information and cultivation.

"My present object is to point out some of the results of mental sterility at a time when society is in the stage which we have been considering. Then, the relations between man and man were summed up in kinship. The fundamental assumption was that all men, not united with you by blood, were your enemies or your slaves. Gradually the assumption became untrue in fact, and men, who were not blood relatives, became related to one another on terms of peace and mutual tolerance or mutual advantage. Yet no new ideas came into being exactly harmonising with the new relation, nor was any new phraseology invented to express it. The new member of each group was spoken of as akin to it, was treated as akin to it, was thought of as akin to it. So little were ideas changed that, as we shall see, the very affections and emotions which the natural bond evoked were called forth in extraordinary strength by the artificial tie. The clear apprehension of these facts throws light on several historical problems, and among them on some of Irish history. Yet they ought not greatly to surprise us, since, in a modified form, they make part of our everyday experience. Almost everybody can observe that, when new circumstances arise, we use our old ideas to bring them home to us; it is only afterwards, and sometimes long afterwards, that our ideas are found to have changed. An English Court of Justice is in great part an engine for working out this process. New combinations of circumstance are constantly arising, but in the first instance they are exclusively interpreted according to old legal ideas. A little later lawyers admit that the old ideas are not quite what they were before the new circumstances arose.

"The slow generation of ideas in ancient times may first be adduced as necessary to the explanation of that great family of Fictions which meet us on the threshold of history and historical jurisprudence."

ESSAY IV

THE CONSTITUTION OF
THE UNITED STATES

The Constitution of the United States of America is much the most important political instrument of modern times. The country, whose destinies it controls and directs, has this special characteristic, that all the territories into which its already teeming population overflows are so placed, that political institutions of the same type can be established in every part of them. The British Empire contains a much larger population, but its portions lie far apart from one another, divided by long stretches of sea, and it is impossible to apply the popular government of the British Islands to all of them, and to none of them can it be applied without considerable modifications. Russia has something like the compactness of the United States, and her population is at present more numerous, although her numbers seem likely to be overtaken in no long time by those included in the American Federation. All the Russian Empire is nominally governed through the sole authority of the Emperor,

but there are already great differences between the
bureaucratic despotism of Western Russia and the military autocracy which presides over the East; and, whenever the crisis comes through which Russian institutions
seem doomed to pass, the difference between the eastern
and western systems of Russian Government cannot fail
to be accentuated. But the United States of America, from
the Atlantic to the Pacific, from the Canadian lakes to the
Mexican border, appear destined to remain for an indefinite time under the same political institutions; and there
is no evidence that these will not continue to belong to
the popular type. Of these institutions, the most important part is defined by the Federal Constitution. The relative importance, indeed, of the Government of the United
States and of the State Governments did not always appear to be as clearly settled as it appears at the present
moment. There was a time at which the authority of the
several States might be thought to be gaining at the expense of the authority of the United States; but the War
of Secession reversed this tendency, and the Federation
is slowly but decidedly gaining at the cost of the States.
Thus, the life and fortunes of the most multitudinous and
homogeneous population in the world will, on the whole
and in the main, be shaped by the Constitution of the
United States.

The political liberty of the United States exercises more
or less influence upon all forms of free government in the
older world. But to us of the present generation it has the
greatest interest for another reason. The success of the
United States has sustained the credit of Republics—a
word which was once used with a good deal of vagueness

to signify a government of any sort without an hereditary king at its head, but which has lately come to have the additional meaning of a government resting on a widely extended suffrage. It is not at all easy to bring home to the men of the present day how low the credit of Republics had sunk before the establishment of the United States. I called attention in my first Essay to the language of contempt in which the writers of the last century speak of the Republics then surviving. The authors of the famous American collection of papers called the *Federalist*, of which I shall have much to say presently, are deeply troubled by the ill-success and ill-repute of the only form of government which was possible for them. The very establishment of their independence had left them a cluster of Republics in the old sense of the word, and, as hereditary kingship was out of the question, their Federal Constitution was necessarily Republican. They tried to take their own Republic out of the class as commonly understood. What they chiefly dreaded was disorder, and they were much impressed by the turbulence, the "fugitive and turbulent existence," of the ancient Republics. But these, they said,[1] were not Republics in the true sense of the name. They were "democracies," commonwealths of the primitive type, governed by the vote of the popular assembly, which consisted of the whole mass of male citizens met together in one place. The true Republic must always be understood as a commonwealth saved from disorder by representative institutions.

But soon after the emancipated Americans began their

---

[1] *Federalist*, No. 10 (Madison).

great experiment, its credit had to be sustained against a much more terrible exemplification of the weaknesses of republican institutions, for the French Republic was established. The black shadow of its crimes still hangs over the century, though it is fading imperceptibly into the distance. But what has not been sufficiently noticed, is its thorough political miscarriage. It tried every expedient by which weak governments, directed by unscrupulous men, attempt to save themselves from open discomfiture. It put to death all who were likely to oppose it, and it conducted its executions on a scale which, for the quantity of blood spilt within narrow limits of time, had been unknown since the Tartar invasions. It tried foreign war, and it obtained success in the field beyond its wildest hopes. It tried military usurpation, and it sent the most distinguished and virtuous of the new constitutional school of French politicians, which was beginning to control it, to perish in tropical swamps. Yet it sank lower and lower into contempt, and died without a struggle. There are not many of the charges brought against Napoleon Bonaparte which are altogether unjust, but he must at any rate be acquitted of having destroyed a Republic, if by a Republic is to be understood a free government. What he destroyed was a military tyranny, for this had been the character of the French Government since the September of 1797; and he substituted for this military tyranny another still severer and infinitely more respected.

As a matter of fact, there is no doubt that the credit of American Republican institutions, and of such institutions generally, did greatly decline through the miserable

issue of the French experiment. The hopes of political
freedom, which the Continental communities were loath
to surrender, turned in another direction, and attached
themselves exclusively to Constitutional Monarchy.
American publicists note the first fifteen years of the
present century as the period during which their country
was least respected abroad and their Government treated
with most contumely by European diplomacy.[2] And just
when the American Federation was overcoming the low
opinion of all Republics which had become common, a
set of events happened close to its doors which might
have overwhelmed it in general shame. The Spanish
Colonies in North, Central, and South America revolted,
and set up Republics in which the crimes and disorders
of the French Republic were repeated in caricature. The
Spanish American Republicans were to the French what
Hébert and Anacharsis Clootz had been to Danton and
Robespierre. This absurd travesty of Republicanism
lasted more than fifty years, and even now the curtain has
not quite fallen upon it. Independently, therefore, of the
history of the United States, it would have seemed quite
certain what the conclusion of political philosophy must
have been upon the various forms of Government as observed under the glass of experience. If we clear our
mental view by adopting the Aristotelian analysis, and
classify all governments as governments of the One,
governments of the Few, and governments of the Many,

---

[2] See the language employed by Canning, as lately as 1821, in conversation
with John Quincy Adams, then American Minister in London (Morse's *Life
of J. Q. Adams*, p. 141).

we shall see that mankind had had much experience of government by the One, and a good deal of government by the Few, and also some very valuable experience of attempts at combining these two forms of Government, but that of government by the Many it had very slight experience, and that whatever it had was on the whole decidedly unfavourable. The antecedent doubt, whether government by the Many was really possible—whether in any intelligible sense, and upon any theory of volition, a multitude of men could be said to have a common will—would have seemed to be strengthened by the fact that, whenever government by the Many had been tried, it had ultimately produced monstrous and morbid forms of government by the One, or of government by the Few. This conclusion would, in truth, have been inevitable, but for the history of the United States, so far as they have had a history. The Federal Constitution has survived the mockery of itself in France and in Spanish America. Its success has been so great and striking, that men have almost forgotten that, if the whole of the known experiments of mankind in government be looked at together, there has been no form of government so unsuccessful as the Republican.

The antecedents of a body of institutions like this, and its mode of growth, manifestly deserve attentive study; and fortunately the materials for the inquiry are full and good. The papers called the *Federalist,* which were published in 1787 and 1788 by Hamilton, Madison, and Jay, but which were chiefly from the pen of Hamilton, were originally written to explain the new Constitution of the United States, then awaiting ratification, and to dispel misconstructions of it which had got abroad. They are thus, undoubtedly, an *ex post facto* defence of the new institutions, but they show us with much clearness either the route by which the strongest minds among the American statesmen of that period had travelled to the conclusions embodied in the Constitution, or the arguments by which they had become reconciled to them. The *Federalist* has generally excited something like enthusiasm in those who have studied it, and among these there have been some not at all given to excessive eulogy. Talleyrand strongly recommended it; and Guizot said of it that, in the application of the elementary principles of government to practical administration, it was the greatest work known to him. An early number of the *Edinburgh Review* (No. 24) described it as a "work little known in Europe, but which exhibits a profundity of research and an acuteness of understanding which would have done honour to the most illustrious statesmen of modern times." The American commendations of the *Federalist* are naturally even less qualified. "I know not," wrote Chancellor Kent, "of any work on the principles of free government that is to be compared in instruction and in intrinsic value to this small and unpretending volume of the *Federalist;* not even if we resort to Aristotle, Cicero, Machiavel, Montesquieu, Milton, Locke, or Burke. It is equally admirable in the depth of its wisdom, the comprehensiveness of its views, the sagacity of its reflections, and the freshness, patriotism, candour, simplicity, and eloquence, with which its truths are uttered and recommended." Those who have attentively read these papers will not think such praise pitched, on the whole, too high. Perhaps the part of it least thoroughly deserved is that given to their supposed profundity of research. There are few traces in the *Federalist* of familiarity with previous speculations on politics, except those of Montesquieu in the *Esprit des Lois*, the popular book of that day. The writers attach the greatest importance to all Montesquieu's opinions. They are much discomposed by his assertion, that Republican government is necessarily associated with a small territory, and they are again comforted by his admission, that this difficulty might be overcome by a confederate Republic. Madison indeed had the acuteness to see that Montesquieu's doctrine is as often polemical as philosophical, and that it is constantly founded on a tacit contrast between the institutions of his own country, which he disliked, with those of England, which he admired. But still his analysis, as we shall hereafter point out, had much influence upon the founders and defenders of the American Constitution. On the whole, Guizot's criticism of the *Federalist* is the most judicious. It is an invaluable work on the application of the elementary principles of government to practical administration. Nothing can be more sagacious than its anticipation of the way in which the new institutions would actually work, or more conclusive than its exposure of the fallacies which underlay the popular objections to some of them.

It is not to be supposed that Hamilton, Jay, and Madison were careless of historical experience. They had made a careful study of many forms of government, ancient and modern. Their observations on the ancient Republics,[3]

---

[3] *Federalist,* No. 14 (Madison).

which were shortly afterwards to prove so terrible a snare to French political theorists, are extremely just. The cluster of commonwealths woven together in the "United Netherlands"[4] is fully examined, and the weaknesses of this anomalous confederacy are shrewdly noted. The remarkable structure of the Romano-German Empire[5] is depicted, and there is reason to suspect that these institutions, now almost forgotten, influenced the framers of the American Constitution, both by attraction and by repulsion. But far the most important experience to which they appealed was that of their own country, at a very recent date. The earliest link had been supplied to the revolted colonies by the first or American "Continental" Congress, which issued the Declaration of Independence. There had subsequently been the "Articles of Confederation," ratified in 1781. These earlier experiments, their demonstrable miscarriage in many particulars, and the disappointments to which they gave rise, are a storehouse of instances and a plentiful source of warning and reflection to the writers who have undertaken to show that their vices are removed in the Constitution of 1787–89.

Nevertheless, there is one fund of political experience upon which the *Federalist* seldom draws, and that is the political experience of Great Britain. The scantiness[6] of

---

[4] *Ibid.,* No. 20 (Hamilton and Madison).

[5] *Ibid.,* No. 19 (Hamilton and Madison). Nos. 19 and 20 are attributed to Hamilton and Madison in Mr. J. C. Hamilton's edition of the *Federalist,* but Hamilton's share in them is not acknowledged in the list left by Madison. See Bancroft, *History of the Formation of the Constitution of the United States,* ii, p. 336.

[6] References to Great Britain occur in *Federalist,* No. 5 (Jay); and (for the purpose of disproving a supposed analogy) in *Federalist,* No. 69 (Hamilton).

these references is at first sight inexplicable. The writers must have understood Great Britain better than any other country, except their own. They had been British subjects during most of their lives. They had scarcely yet ceased to breathe the atmosphere of the British Parliament and to draw strength from its characteristic disturbances. Next to their own stubborn valour, the chief secret of the colonists' success was the incapacity of the English generals, trained in the stiff Prussian system soon to perish at Jena, to adapt themselves to new conditions of warfare, an incapacity which newer generals, full of admiration for a newer German system, were again to manifest at Majuba Hill against a meaner foe. But the colonists had also reaped signal advantage from the encouragements of the British Parliamentary Opposition. If the King of France gave "aid," the English Opposition gave perpetual "comfort" to the enemies of the King of England. It was a fruit of the English party system which was to reappear, amid much greater public dangers, in the Peninsular War; and the revelation of domestic facts, the assertion of domestic weakness, were to assist the arms of a military tyrant, as they had assisted the colonists fighting for independence. Various observations[7] in the *Federalist* on the truculence of party spirit may be suspected of having been prompted by the recollection of what an Opposition can do. But there could be no open reference to this in its pages; and, on the whole, it cannot but be suspected that the fewness of the appeals to British historical examples had its cause in their unpopularity. The object of

---

[7] *Federalist*, No. 70 (Hamilton).

Madison, Hamilton, and Jay was to persuade their countrymen; and the appeal to British experience would only have provoked prejudice and repulsion. I hope, however, to show that the Constitution of the United States is coloured throughout by political ideas of British origin, and that it is in reality a version of the British Constitution, as it must have presented itself to an observer in the second half of the last century.

It has to be carefully borne in mind that the construction of the American Constitution was extremely unlike that process of founding a new Constitution which in our day may be witnessed at intervals of a few years on the European Continent, and that it bore even less resemblance to the foundation of a new Republic, as the word is now understood. Whatever be the occasion of one of these new European Constitutions, be it ill success in war, or escape from foreign dominion, or the overthrow of a government by the army or the mob, the new institutions are always shaped in a spirit of bitter dissatisfaction with the old, which, at the very best, are put upon their trial. But the enfranchised American colonists were more than satisfied with the bulk of their institutions, which were those of the several colonies to which they belonged. And, although they had fought a successful war to get rid of the King of Great Britain and of the British Parliament, they had no quarrel with kings or parliaments as such. Their contention was that the British King and the British Parliament had forfeited by usurpation whatever rights they had, and that they had been justly punished by dispossession. Born free Englishmen, they were not likely to deny the value of parliaments, and, even as to kings, it is probable that many of them had at one time shared the youthful opinion of Alexander Hamilton, who, while totally denying the claim of parliamentary supremacy over the British colonies, except so far as they had conceded it, had argued that the "connecting, pervading principle," necessary to unite a number of individual communities under one common head, could only be found in the person and prerogative of the King, who was "King of America by virtue of a compact between the colonists and the Kings of Great Britain."[8] When once, however, the war had been fought out, and the connection with the Parliament and the King alike had been broken, the business in hand was to supply their place. This new constitutional link had now to be forged from local materials. Among these, there were none for making an hereditary King, hardly any for manufacturing an hereditary Second Chamber; but yet the means of enabling the now separated portion of the British Empire to discharge the functions of a fully organised State, as completely as they had been performed by the kingdom from which it was severed, must somehow be found on the west of the Atlantic. The Constitution of the United States was the fruit of signal sagacity and prescience applied to these necessities. But, again, there was almost no analogy between the new undertaking and the establishment of a modern Continental Republic. The commonwealth founded in America was only called a Republic because it had no hereditary king, and it had no hereditary king because there were no means of having one. At

---

[8] See Preface to J. C. Hamilton's edition of the *Federalist,* p. 10.

that time every community without an hereditary monarchy was considered to be republican. There was a King of Poland elected for life, but his kingdom was styled the Polish Republic. In the style of the elective Romano-German Empire there were still traces of the old Roman Republican Constitution. The Venetian Republic was a stern oligarchy; and, in fact, the elective Doges of Venice and Genoa were as much kings of the old type as those ancient Kings of Rome who originally gave its name to Royal authority. Many of the Swiss Cantons were Republics of the most primitive kind, where the whole population met once a year in assembly to legislate and elect public officers; but one section in some cantons severely governed the others, and some cantons held their dependent territories in the hardest subjection. Now-a-days, however, the establishment of a Republic means the substitution, in all the functions of government, of the Many for the One or the Few—of the totality of the community for a determinate portion of it—an experiment of tremendous and perhaps insuperable difficulty, which the colonists never thought of undertaking. The suffrage, as I shall have to show, was extremely limited in many of the States, and it is unnecessary to state that about half of them were slaveholding communities.

I now propose to take in turn the great Federal institutions set up by the Americans—the President of the United States, the Supreme Court, the Senate, and the House of Representatives—and, in summarily considering them, to point out their relation to pre-existing European, and especially British, institutions. What I may say will perhaps serve in some degree as a corrective of the vague ideas betrayed, not only in the loose phraseology of the English platform, but by the historical common-places of the Americans themselves.

On the face of the Constitution of the United States, the resemblance of the President of the United States to the European King, and especially to the King of Great Britain, is too obvious for mistake. The President has, in various degrees, a number of powers which those who know something of Kingship in its general history recognise at once as peculiarly associated with it and with no other institution. The whole Executive power is vested in him.[9] He is Commander-in-Chief of the Army and Navy.[10] He makes treaties with the advice and consent of the Senate, and with the same advice and consent he appoints Ambassadors, Ministers, Judges, and all high functionaries. He has a qualified veto on legislation. He convenes Congress, when no special time of meeting has been fixed. It is conceded in the *Federalist* that the similarity of the new President's office to the functions of the British King was one of the points on which the opponents of the Constitution fastened. Hamilton replies[11] to their arguments, sometimes with great cogency, sometimes, it must be owned, a little captiously. He urges that the only alternative to a President was a plural Executive, or Council, and he insists on the risk of a paralysis of Executive authority produced by party opposition in such a body. But he mainly relies on the points in

---

[9] C. of U.S. Art. II.

[10] *Ibid.*, 1. 2.

[11] *Federalist*, No. 69 (Hamilton).

which the President differs from the King—on the terminability of the office, on the participation of the Senate in the exercise of several of his powers, on the limited nature of his veto on Bills passed by Congress. It is, however, tolerably clear that the mental operation through which the framers of the American Constitution passed was this: they took the King of Great Britain, went through his powers, and restrained them whenever they appeared to be excessive or unsuited to the circumstances of the United States. It is remarkable that the figure they had before them was not a generalised English king nor an abstract Constitutional monarch; it was no anticipation of Queen Victoria, but George III himself whom they took for their model. Fifty years earlier, or a hundred years later, the English king would have struck them in quite a different light. There had been a tacit compact between the first two Georges and the Whig aristocracy, that the King should govern Hanover and the Whig Ministry Great Britain; and such differences as arose between the King and his subjects were attributable to the fact that European wars began in the Hanoverian department. But George III cared nothing for Hanover and much for governing England. He at once took a new departure in policy by making peace, and setting himself to conduct the government of England in his own way. Now, the original of the President of the United States is manifestly a treaty-making king, and a king actively influencing the Executive Government. Mr. Bagehot insisted that the great neglected fact in the English political system was the government of England by a Committee of the Legislature, calling themselves the Cabinet. This is exactly the method of government to which George III refused to submit, and the framers of the American Constitution take George III's view of the kingly office for granted. They give the whole Executive Government to the President, and they do not permit his Ministers to have seat or speech in either branch of the Legislature. They limit his power and theirs, not, however, by any contrivance known to modern English constitutionalism, but by making the office of President terminable at intervals of four years.

If Hamilton had lived a hundred years later, his comparison of the President with the King would have turned on very different points. He must have conceded that the Republican functionary was much the more powerful of the two. He must have noted that the royal veto on legislation, not thought in 1789 to be quite lost, was irrevocably gone. He must have observed that the powers which the President shared with the Senate had been altogether taken away from the King. The King could make neither war nor treaty; he could appoint neither Ambassador nor Judge; he could not even name his own Ministers. He could do no executive act. All these powers had gone over to Mr. Bagehot's Committee of Parliament. But, a century ago, the only real and essential difference between the Presidential and the Royal office was that the first was not hereditary. The succession of President to President cannot therefore have been copied from Great Britain. But there is no reason to suppose that the method of election was suddenly evolved from the brain of American statesmen. Two features of the original plan have very much fallen out of sight. The President, though ap-

pointed for four years only, was to be indefinitely re-
eligible;[12] the practical limitation of the term of office to
a maximum period of eight years was finally settled only
the other day. And again, the elaborate machinery of
election[13] provided in the Constitution was intended to
be a reality. Each State was to appoint Electors, and the
choice of a President was to be the mature fruit of an
independent exercise of judgment by the electoral college.
Knowing what followed, knowing how thoroughly the
interposition of electors became a futile fiction, and what
was the effect on the character of elections to the Presidency, one cannot but read with some melancholy the
prediction of Hamilton, that "this process of election affords a moral certainty that the office of President will
seldom fall to the lot of any man who is not in an eminent
degree endowed with the requisite qualifications." Understanding, then, that there was to be a real election, by
a selected body, of a President who might conceivably
serve for life, we must recollect that elective Kings had
not died out of Europe. Not long before the War of Independence, at the commencement of the troubles about
the American Stamp Act, a King of the Romans—who,
as Joseph II, turned out to be much more of a Radical
Reformer than ever was George Washington—had been
elected by the Electoral College of the Empire, and the
unfortunate Government called the Polish Republic had
chosen its last King, the luckless Stanislaus Poniatowski.
It seems probable that the framers of the Constitution of

---

[12] *Federalist,* No. 69 (Hamilton).
[13] *Ibid.,* No. 68 (Hamilton).

the United States deliberately rejected the last example, but were to a considerable extent guided by the first. The American Republican Electors are the German Imperial Electors, except that they are chosen by the several States. The writers in the *Federalist* had made an attentive study of the Romano-German Empire, which is analysed in much detail by Hamilton and Madison.[14] They condemn it as a government which can only issue commands to governments themselves sovereign, but not for the mode of electing its executive head. There is some interest in observing that the Electoral Colleges of the United States and of the Empire failed in exactly the same way. The electors fell under the absolute control of the factions dominant in the country. The German electors came to belong[15] to the French or Austrian party, just as the American electors took sides with the Federalists, or with the old Republicans, or with the Whigs, the new Republicans, or the Democrats.

The Supreme Court of the United States, which is the American Federal institution next claiming our attention, is not only a most interesting but a virtually unique creation of the founders of the Constitution. The functions which the Judges of this Court have to discharge under provisions of the Constitution arise primarily from its very nature.[16] The Executive and Legislative authorities

---

[14] *Federalist,* No. 19 (Hamilton and Madison). But see note at p. 205.

[15] The account of the intrigues, French and Austrian, which preceded the election of a king of the Romans forms one of the most amusing portions of the Duc de Broglie's recent work, *Frédéric II et Marie Thérèse.*

[16] See on this subject the valuable remarks of Mr. A. V. Dicey in a paper on "Federal Government," in the first number of the *Law Quarterly Review* (Jan. 1885). Before the Revolution, the British Privy Council had adjudicated on certain questions arising between Colony and Colony.

of the United States have no powers, except such as are expressly conferred on them by the Constitution itself; and, on the other hand, the several States are forbidden by the Constitution to do certain acts and to pass certain laws. What then is to be done if these limitations of power are transgressed by any State, or by the United States? The duty of annulling such usurpations is confided by the Third Article of the Constitution to the Supreme Court, and to such inferior Courts as Congress may from time to time ordain and establish. But this remarkable power is capable only of indirect exercise; it is called into activity by "cases," by actual controversies,[17] to which individuals, or States, or the United States, are parties. The point of unconstitutionality is raised by the arguments in such controversies; and the decision of the Court follows the view which it takes of the Constitution. A declaration of unconstitutionality, not provoked by a definite dispute, is unknown to the Supreme Court.

The success of this experiment has blinded men to its novelty. There is no exact precedent for it, either in the ancient or in the modern world. The builders of Constitutions have of course foreseen the violation of constitutional rules, but they have generally sought for an exclusive remedy, not in the civil, but in the criminal law, through the impeachment of the offender. And, in popular governments, fear or jealousy of an authority not directly delegated by the people has too often caused the difficulty to be left for settlement to chance or to the arbitrament of arms. "Je ne pense pas," wrote De Tocque-

---

[17] *Const. of U.S.*, Art. III., s. 2.

ville, in his *Démocratie en Amérique,* "que jusqu'à présent aucune nation du monde ait constitué le pouvoir judiciaire de la même manière que les Américains."

Yet, novel as was the Federal Judicature established by the American Constitution as a whole, it nevertheless had its roots in the Past, and most of their beginnings must be sought in England. It may be confidently laid down, that neither the institution of a Supreme Court, nor the entire structure of the Constitution of the United States, were the least likely to occur to anybody's mind before the publication of the *Esprit des Lois.* We have already observed that the *Federalist* regards the opinions of Montesquieu as of paramount authority, and no opinion had more weight with its writers than that which affirmed the essential separation of the Executive, Legislative, and Judicial powers. The distinction is so familiar to us, that we find it hard to believe that even the different nature of the Executive and Legislative powers was not recognised till the fourteenth[18] century; but it was not till the eighteenth that the *Esprit des Lois* made the analysis of the various powers of the State part of the accepted political doctrine of the civilised world. Yet, as Madison saw, Montesquieu was really writing of England and contrasting it with France.

The British[19] Constitution was to Montesquieu what Homer has been to the didactic writers on Epic poetry. As the latter have

---

[18] It occurs in the *Defensor Pacis* of the great Chibelline jurist, Marsilio da Padova (1327), with many other curious anticipations of modern political ideas.

[19] *Federalist,* No. 47.

considered the works of the immortal bard the perfect model
from which the principles and rules of the epic art were to be
drawn, and by which all similar works were to be judged, so the
great political critic appears to have viewed the Constitution of
England as the standard, or, to use his own expression, as the
mirror, of political liberty; and to have delivered, in the form of
elementary truths, the several characteristic principles of that
particular system.

The fact was that, in the middle of the eighteenth century, it was quite impossible to say where the respective
provinces of the French King and of the French Parliaments in legislation, and still more of the same authorities
in judicature,[20] began and ended. To this indistinctness
of boundary Montesquieu opposed the considerable but
yet incomplete separation of the Executive, Legislative,
and Judicial powers in England; and he founded on the
contrast his famous generalisation.

Montesquieu adds to his analysis the special proposition, "There is no liberty, if the Judicial power be not
separated from the Legislative and the Executive"; and
here we have, no doubt, the principal source of the provisions of the American Constitution respecting the Federal
Judicature. It is impossible to read the chapter (chap. vi.,
liv. xi.) of the *Esprit des Lois*, in which the words occur,
without perceiving that they must have been suggested
to the writer by what was, on the whole, the English
practice. There were, however, other practices of their
English kinsmen which must have led the framers of the
American Constitution to the same conclusion. They

---

[20] A good account of this confusion is given by M. Louis de Loménie in the
twelfth chapter of his *Beaumarchais et Son Temps.*

must have been keenly alive to the inconvenience of dis-
cussing questions of constitutional law in legislative assemblies. The debates in both Houses of Parliament, from
the accession of George III to the recognition of American
Independence, are astonishingly unlike those of the
present day in one particular. They turn to a surprising
extent on law, and specially on Constitutional law. Everybody in Parliament is supposed to be acquainted with
law, and, above all, the Ministers. The servants of the
Crown may not plead the authority of its Law officers for
their acts; nay, even the Attorney- and Solicitor-General
may not publicly admit that they have been consulted
beforehand, but have to pretend that they are arguing the
legal question before the House on the spur of the moment. There is an apparent survival of these strange fictions in the doctrine which still prevails, that the opinions
of the Law Officers of the Crown are strictly confidential.
During the whole period of the bitter controversies provoked by the grievances of Wilkes and the discontent of
the colonies, it is hard to say whether Parliament or the
Courts of Justice are the proper judges of the points of
law constantly raised. Sometimes a Judge of great eminence speaks with authority, as did Lord Camden on
general warrants, and Lord Mansfield on Wilkes's out-
lawry; but Parliament is just as often the field to which
the perpetual strife is transferred. The confusion reaches
its height when Lord Chatham in the House of Lords
declares the House of Commons to be open to a civil
action for not giving Wilkes a seat, when Lord Mansfield
covers this opinion with ridicule, and when Lord Camden
to some extent supports Lord Chatham. These are the true

causes of the unsatisfactory condition of English Constitutional law, and of its many grave and dangerous uncer-
tainties.

The impression made on American minds by a system
under which legal questions were debated with the utmost acrimony, but hardly ever solved, must have been
deepened by their familiarity with the very question at
issue between the mother-country and the colonies. On
this question Englishmen, content as is their wont with
the rough rule of success or failure as the test of right or
wrong in national undertakings, have generally accepted
the view which was, on the whole, that of the Whig
Opposition. And it must be allowed that the statesmen
of the most unpopular country in Europe ought to have
known that it could not attempt to subdue a great and
distant dependency, without bringing its most powerful
European enemies on its back. As for American opinion,
the merits of the issue have been buried deep in the
nauseous grandiloquence of the American panegyrical
historians. Yet, in reality, the question was in the highest
degree technical, in the highest degree difficult, in the
highest degree fitted for adjudication by an impartial
Court, if such a tribunal could have been imagined. What
was the exact significance of the ancient constitutional
formula which connected taxation with representation?
When broadly stated by the colonists, it must have struck
many Englishmen of that day as a mischievous paradox,
since it seemed to deny the right of Parliament to tax, not
only Massachusetts, but Manchester and Birmingham,
which were not represented in any intelligible sense in
the House of Commons. On the other hand, the American

contention is largely accounted for by the fact, that the local assemblies in which the colonists were represented "were not formally instituted, but grew up by themselves, because it was in the nature of Englishmen to assemble."[21] They were a natural product of soil once become British. The truth is that, from the popular point of view, either the affirmation or the denial of the moot point led straight to an absurdity; and when the dispute was over, its history must have suggested to thoughtful men, who had once recovered their calmness, the high expediency of judicial mediation in questions between State and State acknowledging the same sovereignty.

Let me finally note that the Constitution of the United States imposes (Art. III., s. 2) on the Judges of the Supreme Court a method of adjudication which is essentially English. No general proposition is laid down by the English tribunal, unless it arises on the facts of the actual dispute submitted to it for adjudication. The success of the Supreme Court of the United States largely results from its following this mode of deciding questions of constitutionality and unconstitutionality. The process is slower, but it is freer from suspicion of pressure, and much less provocative of jealousy, than the submission of broad and emergent political propositions to a judicial body; and this submission is what an European foreigner thinks of when he contemplates a Court of Justice decid-

---

[21] See Seeley, *The Expansion of England.* Professor Seeley, at p. 67 of this excellent book, quotes from Hutchinson the statement: "This year (1619) a House of Burgesses *broke out* in Virginia."

ing on alleged violations of a constitutional rule or principle.

The Congress or Legislature of the United States, sharply separated from the Executive in conformity with Montesquieu's principle, consists, I need scarcely say, of the Senate and the House of Representatives. And here I follow Mr. Freeman in noting this two-chambered legislature as a plain mark of the descent of the American Federal Constitution, as it was at an earlier date of the descent of American Colonial Constitutions, from a British original. If we could conceive a political architect of the eighteenth century endeavouring to build a new Constitution in ignorance of the existence of the British Parliament, or with the deliberate determination to neglect it, he might be supposed to construct his Legislature with one Chamber, or three, or four; he would have been in the highest degree unlikely to construct it with two. The *Federalist,* no doubt, seems[22] to regard the Senates of the ancient world as in some sense Second Chambers of a Legislature, but these peculiar bodies, originally consisting of the old men of the community, would have been found on closer inspection to answer very slightly to this conception.[23] The first real anticipation of a Second Chamber, armed with a veto on the proposals of a separate authority, and representing a different interest, occurs in that much-misunderstood institution, the Roman Tribunate. In the modern feudal world, the community naturally distributed itself into classes or Estates, and

---

[22] *Federalist,* No. 63 (Hamilton).
[23] See Maine, *Early Law and Custom,* pp. 24, 25.

there are abundant traces of legislatures in which these classes were represented according to various principles. But the Estates of the Realm were grouped in all sorts of ways. In France, the States-General were composed of three orders, the Clergy, the Nobility, and the rest of the Nation as the Tiers État. There were three orders also in Spain. In Sweden there were four, the Clergy, the Nobility, the Burghers, and the Peasants. The exceptional two Houses of the British Constitution arose from special causes. The separate Parliamentary representation of the Clergy came early to an end in England, except so far the great dignitaries of the Church were summoned to the House of Lords; and the Knights of the Shire, who represented the great mass of landed proprietors, were disjoined from the nobility, and sat with the representatives of the towns in the House of Commons.

The Senate of the United States, constituted under section 3 of the First Article of the Federal Constitution, is at this moment one of the most powerful political bodies in the world. In point of dignity and authority, it has in no wise disappointed the sanguine expectations of its founders. As I have already said, it is not possible to compare the predictions of the *Federalist* with the actual history of the Presidency of the United States, without being forced to acknowledge that in this particular the hopes of Hamilton and his coadjutors have failed of fulfilment. But the Senate has, on the whole, justified the hopes of it which they expressed.

> Through the medium of the State legislatures, which are select bodies of men, and who are to appoint the members of the National Senate, there is reason to expect that this branch will

generally be composed with peculiar care and judgment; that these circumstances promise greater knowledge and more comprehensive information in the national annals; and that, on account of the extent of country from which will be drawn those to whose direction they will be committed, they will be less apt to be tainted by the spirit of faction, and more out of the reach of those occasional ill-humours, or temporary prejudices and propensities, which in smaller societies frequently contaminate the public deliberations, beget injustice and oppression towards a part of the community, and engender schemes which, though they gratify a momentary inclination or desire, terminate in general distress, dissatisfaction, and disgust.[24]

We may not reasonably doubt that the Senate is indebted for its power—a power which has rather increased than diminished since the Federal Constitution came into force—and for its hold on the public respect, to the principles upon which it was deliberately founded, to the mature age of the Senators, to their comparatively long tenure of office, which is for six years at least, and above all to the method of their election by the Legislatures of the several States.

It is very remarkable that the mode of choosing the Senate finally adopted did not commend itself to some of the strongest minds employed on the construction of the Federal Constitution. Its First Article provides (in s. 3) that "the Senate of the United States shall be composed of two Senators from each State, chosen by the Legislatures thereof, for six years." Hence it follows that the Senate is a political body, of which the basis is not equality, but inequality. Each State elects no more and no fewer than two Senators. Rhode Island, Delaware, and Mary-

---

[24] *Federalist,* No. 27 (Hamilton).

land have the same representation in the Senate, as the great and populous States of New York and Pennsylvania. The Constitutional composition of the Senate is therefore a negation of equality. Now, the writer whose prediction I quoted above is Alexander Hamilton, and Hamilton himself had proposed a very different mode of constituting a Senate. His plan had been that the Senate should consist of "persons to be chosen by Electors, elected for that purpose by the citizens and inhabitants of the several States who shall have in their own right, or in right of their wives, an estate in land for not less than life, or a term of years whereof, at the time of giving their votes, there shall be at least fourteen years unexpired." The scheme further provided that each Senator should be elected from a District, and that the number of Senators should be apportioned between the different States according to a rule roughly representing population. The blended political and economical history of Europe has now shown us that Hamilton's plan would not, in all probability, have proved durable. It is founded on inequality of property, and specially on inequality of landed property. We are now, however, in a position to lay down, as the result of experience and observation, that, although popular government has steadily extended itself in the Western world, and although liberty is the parent of inequalities in fortune, these inequalities are viewed by democratic societies with a peculiar jealousy, and that no form of property is so much menaced in such societies as property in land. When the Federal Constitution was framed, there were property qualifications for voting in the greater number of the American states, and it will be seen that these limitations of the suffrage were allowed to have influence in the House of Representatives. But they have given way almost everywhere to a suffrage very little short of universal, and the foundation of Hamilton's Senate would probably have undergone a similar change. Nevertheless, though inequalities of fortune are resented by modern democracy, historical inequalities do not appear to be resented in the same degree—possibly to some extent because the consideration which Science has finally secured for the heredity of the individual has insensibly extended to the heredity of commonwealths. Now the Senate of the United States reflects the great fact of their history, the original political equality of the several States. Since the War of Secession and its event in the triumph of the North, this fact has become purely historical; but it illustrates all the more an apparent inference from modern European experiments in constitution-building—from the actual history in Europe of Constitutional Kings, Presidents of a Republic, and Second Legislative Chambers—that nothing but an historical principle can be successfully opposed to the principle of making all public powers and all parliamentary assemblies the mere reflection of the average opinion of the multitude. On all questions connected with the Federal Senate, Hamilton unconsciously took the less Conservative side. Not only would he have distinguished the electoral body choosing the Senate from the electoral body choosing the House of Representatives by a property qualification solely, but he would have annulled from the first the self-government of the States by giving the appointment of the Governor or President of each separate State to Federal authority.[25]

The House of Representatives, which shares with the Senate the legislative powers of the United States, is unquestionably a reproduction of the House of Commons. No Constitution but the British could have suggested section 7 of Article I of the Federal Constitution, which lays down a British principle, and settles a dispute which had arisen upon it in a particular way. "All Bills raising Revenue shall originate in the House of Representatives; but the Senate may propose or concur with amendments as in other Bills." There is a common impression in this country, that the American House of Representatives was somehow intended to be a more democratic assembly than our House of Commons. But this is a vulgar error. The Constitutional provision on the subject is contained in section 2 of the First Article, which is to the effect that the House is to be composed of members chosen every second year by the people of the several States, and that the electors in each State are to "have the qualifications requisite for Electors of the most numerous branch of the State Legislature." The *Federalist* expressly tells us that the differences in the qualification were at that time "very material." "In every State," it adds,[26] "a certain proportion of the inhabitants are deprived of this right by the Constitution of the State." Nor

---

[25] Alexander Hamilton's scheme of a Constitution is printed at page 31 of Mr. J. C. Hamilton's edition of the *Federalist.*

[26] *Federalist,* No. 54 (Hamilton).

had the provision for biennial elections the significance which would have been attached to it at a later date. Our present ideas have been shaped by the Septennial Act, but it is quite evident that in Hamilton's day the Septennial Act was still regarded as a gross usurpation, and that the proper English system was thought to be one of triennial Parliaments. Election every two years seems to have been taken as a fair mean between the systems of the States which made up the Federation. There were septennial elections in Virginia, which had been one of the most forward of the States in pressing on the Revolution; but in Connecticut and Rhode Island there were actually half-yearly elections, and annual elections in South Carolina.

The House of Representatives is a much more exclusively legislative body than either the Senate of the United States or than the present British House of Commons. Many of the Executive powers vested in the President cannot be exercised save with the consent of the Senate. And, as the Congress has not yet repealed the legislation by which it sought to trammel the recalcitrant President, Andrew Johnson, after the War of Secession, the Executive authority of the Senate is now probably wider than it was ever intended to be by the framers of the Constitution. The House of Representatives has no similar rights over the province of the Executive; and this restriction of power is itself a feature connecting it with the British House of Commons, as known to the American statesmen of the Revolution. The far-reaching and perpetual interference with the Executive Government, which is now exercised by the House of Commons through the interrogation of the Ministers, was then at most in its first feeble beginnings; and moreover the right of the House to designate the public servants, who are nominally the Ministers of the Crown, had for a considerable time been successfully disputed by the King. George I and George II had, on the whole, carried out the understanding that their Ministers should be taken from a particular class; but George III had conducted the struggle with the Colonists through servants of his own choosing, and, when the Americans were framing their Constitution, he had established his right for the rest of his reign. It is to be observed that the Constitution of the United States settles the quarrel in the sense contended for by the King of England. The heads of the Executive Departments subordinated to the President do not sit in the Senate or in the House. They are excluded from both by section 6 of Article I, which provides that "no person holding any office under the United States shall be a member of either House during his continuance in office."

We are here brought to one of the most interesting subjects which can engage the attention of the Englishman of our day, the points of difference between the Government of the United States, as it works under the provisions of the Federal Constitution, and the Government of Great Britain as it has developed itself independently of any express controlling instrument. In order to bring out a certain number of these differences clearly, I will first describe the manner in which the American House of Representatives carries on its legislation, and its method of regulating that occasional contact between the Executive authorities and the Legislature, which is inseparable from free government. I will then contrast the system with that which is followed by the British House of Commons at this moment. The difference will be found to be striking, and, to an Englishman, perhaps disquieting.

The House of Representatives distributes itself, under its Tenth Rule, into no less than forty Standing Committees, independently of Joint-Committees of Senators and Representatives. The subjects over which these Committees have jurisdiction comprise the whole business of Government, from Financial, Foreign, and Military Affairs, to the Codification of the Law and the Expenditure on Public Buildings. The Eleventh Rule provides that "all proposed legislation shall be referred to the Committees named in the Tenth Rule." As there are no officials in the House, all Bills are necessarily introduced by private members, who draft them as they please. I believe that, practically, every such Bill is allowed to go to the appropriate Committee, but that the proportion of them which are "reported" by the Committees and come back to the House is extremely small. Lawyers abound in the House, and the Committee, in fact, re-draws the Bill. Every measure, therefore, has its true beginning in the bosom of a strictly legislative body. How this contrasts with the early stages of British legislation will be seen presently. The differences in the mode of contact between the House and the Executive Departments differ still more widely in the two countries. This contact is governed in the United States by the Twenty-fourth Rule of the House. First of all, if information be required from the Secretary of State or other Ministers, a resolution of the House must be obtained. Once a week, under the Rule, and on that occasion only, "resolutions of inquiry directed to the heads of the Executive Departments shall be in order for reference to appropriate Committees, which resolutions shall be reported to the House within one week thereafter." Sometimes, I believe, the Minister attends the Committee; but, if he pleases, he may answer the resolution by a formal communication addressed to the Speaker of the House. This carefully guarded procedure answers to the undefined and irregular practice of putting and answering questions in our own House of Commons.

The procedure of the American House of Representatives, both in respect of the origination of bills and of the interrogation of Ministers, is that of a political body which considers that its proper functions are not executive, but legislative. The British House of Commons, on the other hand, which the greatest part of the world regards as a legislative assembly (though it never quite answered to that description), has, since 1789, taken under its supervision and control the entire Executive government of Great Britain, and much of the government of her colonies and dependencies. There are no theoretical limits to its claim for official information, not merely concerning general lines of policy, but concerning the minute details of administration. It gives effect to its claim by questions put publicly to Ministers on the Treasury Bench, and, independently of all other results of this practice, the mere time consumed by the multitude of questions and replies is beginning to encroach very seriously on the time available for legislation. A singularly small number of these questions appear to have their origin in the interest which a member of the House of Commons may legitimately feel in foreign and domestic policy. Some, no doubt, spring from innocent curiosity; some from pardonable vanity; but not a few are deliberately intended to work public mischief. It is a minor objection, that the number of questions which are flagrantly argumentative is manifestly increasing.

All legislative proposals which have any serious chance of becoming law, proceed in the United States from Committees of the Senate or of the House of Representatives. Where are we to place the birth of an English legislative measure? He who will give his mind to this question will find it one of the obscurest which ever perplexed the political observer. Some Bills undoubtedly have their origin in the Executive Departments, where the vices of existing laws or systems have been disclosed in the process of actual administration. Others may be said to be conceived in the House of Commons, having for their embryo either the Report of a Committee of the House or of a resolution passed by it which, according to a modern practice, suggested no doubt by the difficulties of legislation, has taken the place of the private member's Bill. But if we may trust the experience of 1883, by far the most important measures, measures fraught with the gravest consequence to the whole future of the nation, have a much more remarkable beginning. One of the great English political parties, and naturally the party supporting the Government in power, holds a Conference of gentlemen, to whom I hope I may without offence apply the American name "wire-pullers," and this Conference dictates to the Government, not only the legislation which it is to submit to the House of Commons, but the order in which it is to be submitted. Here we are introduced to the great modern paradox of the British Constitution. While the House of Commons has assumed the supervision of the whole Executive Government, it has turned over to the Executive Government the most important part of the business of legislation. For it is in the Cabinet that the effective work of legislation begins. The Ministers, hardly recruited from the now very serious fatigues of a Session which lasts all but to the commencement of September, assemble in Cabinet in November, and in the course of a series of meetings, extending over rather more than a fortnight, determine what legislative proposals are to be submitted to Parliament. These proposals, sketched, we may believe, in not more than outline, are then placed in the hands of the Government draftsman; and, so much is there in all legislation which consists in the manipulation of detail and in the adaptation of vaguely conceived novelties to pre-existing law, that we should not probably go far wrong if we attributed four-fifths of every legislative enactment to the accomplished lawyer who puts into shape the Government Bills. From the measures which come from his hand, the tale of Bills to be announced in the Queen's Speech is made up, and at this point English legislation enters upon another stage.

The American political parties of course support and oppose particular legislative measures. They are elated at the success of a particular Bill, and disappointed by its failure. But no particular consequences beyond disappointment follow the rejection of a Bill. The Government of the country goes on as before. In England it is otherwise. Every Bill introduced into Parliament by the Ministry (and we have seen that all the really important Bills are thus introduced) must be carried through the House of Commons without substantial alteration, or the Ministers will resign, and consequences of the gravest kind may follow in the remotest parts of an empire extending to the ends of the earth. Thus a Government Bill has to be forced through the House of Commons with the whole strength of party organisation, and in a shape very closely resembling that which the Executive Government gave to it. It should then in strictness pass through a searching discussion in the House of Lords; but this stage of English legislation is becoming merely nominal, and the judgment on it of the Crown has long since become a form. It is therefore the Executive Government which should be credited with the authorship of English legislation. We have thus an extraordinary result. The nation whose constitutional practice suggested to Montesquieu his memorable maxim concerning the Executive, Legislative, and Judicial powers, has in the course of a century falsified it. The formal Executive is the true source of legislation; the formal Legislature is incessantly concerned with Executive Government.

After its first birth, nothing can be more equable and nothing can be more plain to observation than the course of an American legislative measure. A Bill, both in the House of Representatives and the Senate, goes through an identical number of stages of about equal length. When it has passed both Houses, it must still commend itself to the President of the United States, who has a veto on it which, though qualified, is constantly used, and is very difficult to overcome. An English Bill begins in petty rivulets or stagnant pools. Then it runs underground for most of its course, withdrawn from the eye by the secrecy of the Cabinet. Emerging into the House of Commons, it can no more escape from its embankments than the water of a canal; but once dismissed from that House, it overcomes all remaining obstacles with the rush of a cataract, and mixes with the trackless ocean of British institutions.

The very grave dangers entailed on our country by this eccentric method of legislation arise from its being followed, not only in the enactment of ordinary laws, but in the amendment of what, if it be still permitted to us to employ the word, is called the British Constitution. "En Angleterre," writes De Tocqueville, "la Constitution peut changer sans cesse; *ou plutôt elle n'existe pas.*" There are doubtless strong Conservative forces still surviving in England; they survive because, though our political institutions have been transformed, the social conditions out of which they originally grew are not extinct. But of all the infirmities of our Constitution in its decay, there is none more serious than the absence of any special precautions to be observed in passing laws which touch the very foundations of our political system. The nature of this weakness, and the character of the manifold and elaborate securities which are contrasted with it in America, may be well illustrated by considering two famous measures—the Reform of the London Corporation, which is still unaccomplished, and the County Franchise Bill, now become law. The reconstruction of the London

Municipality, though a very difficult undertaking, would belong in America to the ordinary State Legislatures. The Legislature of New York State has, in fact, several times attempted to remodel the municipality of New York City, which has repeatedly shown itself to be corrupt, unmanageable, and inefficient; and these attempts call for no special remark, except that they have hitherto met with only the most moderate success. But a measure distantly resembling the English County Franchise Bill would be, both from the point of view of the several States and from the point of view of the United States, a Constitutional amendment. In the least considerable, the least advanced, and the most remote American State, its enactment would have to be coupled with the carefully devised precautionary formalities which I described in the latter part of the Second Essay. If an American County Franchise Bill were proposed to be enforced by Federal authority, the designed difficulty of carrying it would be vastly greater. As a rule, the Federal Constitution does not interfere with the franchise; it leaves the right of voting to be regulated by the several States, gradually and locally, according to the varying circumstances of each, and the political views prevailing in it. But the rule has now been departed from in the new Article, securing the suffrage to the negroes; and there is no question that, if a measure were contemplated in America, bearing to the entirety of American institutions the same relation which the County Franchise Bill bore to the entirety of ours—nay, even if a simple change in the franchise had to be introduced into all the States, or into the bulk of them, simultaneously—the object could only be effected by an amendment of the Constitution of the United States. It would therefore have to be dealt with under the Fifth Article of the Constitution. This article, which is the keystone of the whole Federal fabric, runs as follows:

> The Congress, whenever two-thirds of both Houses shall deem it necessary, shall propose Amendments to this Constitution; or, on the application of the Legislatures of two-thirds of the several States, shall call a Convention for proposing Amendments which, in either case, shall be valid to all intents and purposes as part of this Constitution, when ratified by the Legislatures of three-fourths of the several States or by Conventions in three-fourths thereof, as one or the other mode of ratification may be proposed by the Congress.

The mode, therefore, of proceeding with a measure requiring an amendment of the Constitution would be this. First of all, the Senate of the United States and the House of Representatives must resolve, by a two-thirds majority of each Chamber, that the proposed amendment is desirable. The amendment has then to be ratified by the Legislatures of three-fourths of the several States. Now, there are at the present moment thirty-eight States in the American Union. The number of Legislatures which must join in the ratification is therefore twenty-nine. I believe, however, that there is no State in which the Legislature does not consist of two Houses, and we arrive, therefore, at the surprising result that, before a constitutional measure of the gravity of the English County Franchise Bill could become law in the United States, it must have at the very least in its favor the concurring vote of no less than fifty-eight separate legislative chambers, independently of the Federal Legislature, in which a double two-thirds majority must be obtained. The alternative course permitted by the Constitution, of calling separate special Conventions of the United States and of the several States, would prove probably in practice even lengthier and more complicated.

The great strength of these securities against hasty innovation has been shown beyond the possibility of mistake by the actual history of the Federal Constitution. On March 4, 1789, the day fixed for commencing the operation of the new Federal Government, the Constitution had been ratified by all the States then established, except three. One of the first acts of the new Congress was to propose to the States, on September 25, 1789, a certain number of amendments on comparatively unimportant points, which had no doubt been suggested by the discussions on the draft-Constitution, and the several States ratified these amendments in the course of the following year. An amendment of more importance, relating to the power of the Supreme Court, was declared to have been ratified on September 5, 1794; and another, remedying a singular inconvenience which had disclosed itself in the original rule regulating the election of the President and of the Vice-President, had its ratification completed in September 1804. After these early amendments, which were comparatively easy of adoption through the small number of the original States, there was no change in the Federal Constitution for sixty years. The Thirteenth, Fourteenth, and Fifteenth Amendments, which became part of the Constitution in the period between the beginning of 1865 and the beginning of 1870, were the fruits of the conquest of the South by the North. They abolish slavery, provide against its revival, forbid the abridgment of the right to vote on the ground of race or colour, impose penalties on the vanquished adherents of the seceding States, and incidentally give a constitutional guarantee to the Public Debt of the Federation. But they could not have been either proposed or ratified, if the South had not lain under the heel of the North. The military forces of the United States controlled the Executive Governments of the Southern States, and virtually no class of the population, except the negroes, was represented in the Southern Legislatures. The War of Secession, which was itself a war of Revolution, was in fact succeeded by a Revolutionary period of several years, during which not only the institutions of the Southern States, but the greater part of the Federal institutions were more or less violently distorted to objects not contemplated by the framers of the Constitution. But the form of the Federal institutions was always preserved, and they gradually recovered their reality, until at the present moment the working of the Constitution of the United States does not, save for the disappearance of negro slavery, differ from the mode of its operation before the civil convulsion of 1861–65.

The powers and disabilities attached to the United States and to the several States by the Federal Constitution, and placed under the protection of the deliberately contrived securities we have described, have determined the whole course of American history. That history began, as all its records abundantly show, in a condition of society produced by war and revolution, which might have condemned the great Northern Republic to a fate not unlike that of her disorderly sisters in South America. But the provisions of the Constitution have acted on her like those dams and dykes which strike the eye of the traveller along the Rhine, controlling the course of a mighty river which begins amid mountain torrents, and turning it into one of the most equable waterways in the world. The English Constitution, on the other hand, like the great river of England, may perhaps seem to the observer to be now-a-days always more or less in flood, owing to the crumbling of the banks and the water poured into it from millions of drain-pipes. The observation is, however, worth making, that the provisions of the Constitution of the United States which have most influenced the destinies of the American people are not always those which the superficial student of it would first notice. Attention is easily attracted by Article IV, section 4, which makes the United States guarantee to every State in the Union a Republican form of government, and, on the other hand, protection against domestic violence; and again, by sections 9 and 10 of Article I, which prohibit the United States and the several States from granting titles of Nobility. No man can mistake the importance of the portions of the First Article which forbid the several States to enter into any treaty, alliance, or confederation, to make anything but gold or silver coin a tender in payment of debts, and (without the consent of Congress) to keep troops or ships of war in time of peace. But a hasty reader might under-estimate the practical effects of the provisions in Article I which empower the United States "to promote the progress of science and the useful arts, by securing for limited times to authors and inventors the exclusive right to their respective writings and discoveries," and, again, of the parts of the same Article which prohibit the United States and the several States from laying any tax or duty on articles exported from any State; and, lastly, of the remarkable provision which forbids a State to pass any law impairing the obligation of contracts. The power to grant patents by Federal authority has, however, made the American people the first in the world for the number and ingenuity of the inventions by which it has promoted the "useful arts"; while, on the other hand, the neglect to exercise this power for the advantage of foreign writers has condemned the whole American community to a literary servitude unparalleled in the history of thought. The prohibition against levying duties on commodities passing from State to State is again the secret both of American Free-trade and of American Protection. It secures to the producer the command of a free market over an enormous territory of vast natural wealth, and thus it secondarily reconciles the American people to a tariff on foreign importations as oppressive as ever a nation has submitted to. I have seen the rule which denies to the several States the power to make any laws impairing the obligation of contracts criticised as if it were a mere politico-economical flourish; but in point of fact there is no more important provision in the whole Constitution. Its principle was much extended by a decision of the Supreme Court,[27] which ought now to interest a large number of Englishmen, since it is the basis of the credit of many of the great

---

[27] In *Dartmouth College* v. *Woodward,* a case argued by Daniel Webster in 1818.

American Railway Incorporations. But it is this prohibition which has in reality secured full play to the economical forces by which the achievement of cultivating the soil of the North American Continent has been performed; it is the bulwark of American individualism against democratic impatience and Socialistic fantasy. We may usefully bear in mind that, until this prohibition, as interpreted by the Federal Courts, is got rid of, certain communistic schemes of American origin, which are said to have become attractive to the English labouring classes because they are supposed to proceed from the bosom of a democratic community, have about as much prospect of obtaining practical realisation in the United States as the vision of a Cloud-Cuckooborough to be built by the birds between earth and sky.

It was not to be expected that all the hopes of the founders of the American Constitution would be fulfilled. They do not seem to have been prepared for the rapid development of party, chiefly under the influence of Thomas Jefferson, nor for the thorough organisation with which the American parties before long provided themselves. They may have expected the House of Representatives, which is directly elected by the people, to fall under the dominion of faction, but the failure of their mechanism for the choice of a President was a serious disappointment. I need hardly say that the body intended to be a true Electoral College has come to consist of mere duties of the two great contending parties, and that a Presidential Elector has no more active part in choosing a President than has a balloting paper. The miscarriage has told upon the qualities of American Presidents. An

Electoral College may commit a blunder, but a candidate for the Presidency, nominated for election by the whole people, will, as a rule, be a man selected because he is not open to obvious criticism, and will therefore in all probability be a mediocrity. But, although the President of the United States has not been all which Washington and Hamilton, Madison and Jay, intended him to be, nothing has occurred in America to be compared with the distortion which the Presidency has suffered at the hands of its copyists on the European Continent. It is probable that no foreigner but an Englishman can fully understand the Constitution of the United States, though even an Englishman is apt to assume it to have been much more of a new political departure than it really was, and to forget to compare it with the English institutions of a century since. But, while it has made the deepest possible impression on Continental European opinion, it has been hardly ever comprehended. Its imitators have sometimes made the historical mistake of confounding the later working of some of its parts with that originally intended by its founders. And sometimes they have fallen into the practical error of attempting to combine its characteristics with some of the modern characteristics of the British Constitution. The President of the Second French Republic was directly elected by the French people in conformity with the modern practice of the Americans, and the result was that, confident in the personal authority witnessed to by the number of his supporters, he overthrew the Republic and established a military despotism. The President of the Third French Republic is elected in a different and safer way; but the Ministers whom he appoints have seats in the French Legislature, mix in its debates, and are responsible to the Lower House, just as are the members of an English Cabinet. The effect is, that there is no living functionary who occupies a more pitiable position than a French President. The old Kings of France reigned and governed. The Constitutional King, according to M. Thiers, reigns, but does not govern. The President of the United States governs, but he does not reign. It has been reserved for the President of the French Republic neither to reign nor yet to govern.

The Senate has proved a most successful institution except in one particular. Congress includes many honourable as well as very many able men, but it would be affectation to claim for the American Federal Legislature as a whole that its hands are quite clean. It is unnecessary to appeal on this point to satire or fiction; the truth is, that too many Englishmen have been of late years concerned with Congressional business for there to be any want of evidence that much money is spent in forwarding it which is not legitimately expended. One provision of the Constitution has here defeated another. One portion of the 6th section of the First Article provides securities against corruption on the part of Senators and Representatives, but the portion immediately preceding provides that "Senators and Representatives shall have a compensation for their services, to be ascertained by law and paid out of the Treasury of the United States." This system of payment for legislative services, which prevails throughout the whole of the Union, has produced a class of professional politicians, whose probity in some cases has proved unequal to the strain put upon it by the power

of dealing with the public money and the public posses-
sions of what will soon be the wealthiest community in
the world. It is a point of marked inferiority to the British
political system, even in its decline.

It may be thought that a great American institution
failed on one occasion conspicuously and disastrously.
The Supreme Court of the United States did not succeed
in preventing by its mediation the War of Secession. But
the inference is not just. The framers of the Constitution
of the United States, like succeeding generations of
American statesmen, deliberately thrust the subject of
Slavery as far as they could out of their own sight. It
barely discloses itself in the method of counting population for the purpose of fixing the electoral basis of the
House of Representatives, and in the subsequently famous provision of the Fourth Article, that persons
"bound to service or labour in one State" shall be delivered up if they escape into another. But, on the whole,
the makers of the Constitution pass by on the other side.
They have not the courage of their opinions, whatever
they were. They neither guarantee Slavery on the one
hand, nor attempt to regulate it on the other, or to provide
for its gradual extinction. When then, about seventy
years afterwards, the Supreme Court was asked to decide
whether the owner of slaves taking them into one of the
territories of the Union, not yet organised as a State,
retained his right of ownership, it had not in reality sufficient materials for a decision. The grounds of its judgment
in the *Dred Scott* case may have been perhaps satisfactory
to lawyers, but in themselves they satisfied nobody else.
It is extremely significant that, in the one instance in

which the authors of the Constitution declined of set purpose to apply their political wisdom to a subject which they knew to be all-important, the result was the bloodiest and costliest war of modern times.

Let me repeat the points which I trust I have done something towards establishing. The Constitution of the United States is a modified version of the British Constitution; but the British Constitution which served as its original was that which was in existence between 1760 and 1787. The modifications introduced were those, and those only, which were suggested by the new circumstances of the American Colonies, now become independent. These circumstances excluded an hereditary king, and virtually excluded an hereditary nobility. When the American Constitution was framed, there was no such sacredness to be expected for it as before 1789 was supposed to attach to all parts of the British Constitution. There was every prospect of political mobility, if not of political disorder. The signal success of the Constitution of the United States in stemming these tendencies is, no doubt, owing in part to the great portion of the British institutions which were preserved in it; but it is also attributable to the sagacity with which the American statesmen filled up the interstices left by the inapplicability of certain of the then existing British institutions to the emancipated colonies. This sagacity stands out in every part of the *Federalist,* and it may be tracked in every page of subsequent American history. It may well fill the Englishmen who now live *in fæce Romuli* with wonder and envy.

Index

COLOPHON

This book is printed on 70-pound long-fibre, acid-free paper especially developed by the S. D. Warren Company to meet the historical document standards of the United States National Historical Publications and Records Commission.

The Compano typeface used in this volume is a computer-assisted typeface that matches the Palatino typeface which is the work of Hermann Zapf, the noted European type designer and master calligrapher. Palatino is basically an "old style" letterform, yet strongly endowed with the Zapf distinction of exquisiteness. With concern not solely for the individual letter but also the working visual relationship in a page of text, Zapf's edged pen has given this type a brisk, natural motion.

Book design by Design Center, Inc., Indianapolis
Typography by Kingsport Press, Kingsport, Tennessee
Printed by Kingsport Press, Kingsport, Tennessee